This material generously provided by
The Library Foundation of Hillsboro
Courtesy of:

2011 ENDOWMENT

MISSION
STATEMENT

*To foster and reflect community
commitment to education and the
pursuit of knowledge by providing
access and opportunities, through
advocacy and financial support of
the Hillsboro Public Library;
and*

*To educate, encourage, enrich and
enlighten the population by
enhancing collections, technology,
services, and facilities of the
Hillsboro Public Library.*

For information about the Library
Foundation of Hillsboro and its
endowment programs contact the
Library Director.

2850 NE Brookwood Parkway
Hillsboro, Oregon 97124-5327
503/615-6500

TRANSFORMATIVE
ENTREPRENEURS

TRANSFORMATIVE ENTREPRENEURS

HOW WALT DISNEY, STEVE JOBS, MUHAMMAD YUNUS, AND OTHER INNOVATORS SUCCEEDED

JEFFREY A. HARRIS

palgrave
macmillan

HILLSBORO PUBLIC LIBRARIES
Hillsboro, OR
Member of Washington County
COOPERATIVE LIBRARY SERVICES

TRANSFORMATIVE ENTREPRENEURS
Copyright © Jeffrey A. Harris, 2012.

All rights reserved.

First published in 2012 by
PALGRAVE MACMILLAN®
in the United States—a division of St. Martin's Press LLC,
175 Fifth Avenue, New York, NY 10010.

Where this book is distributed in the UK, Europe and the rest of the world,
this is by Palgrave Macmillan, a division of Macmillan Publishers Limited,
registered in England, company number 785998, of Houndmills,
Basingstoke, Hampshire RG21 6XS.

Palgrave Macmillan is the global academic imprint of the above companies
and has companies and representatives throughout the world.

Palgrave® and Macmillan® are registered trademarks in the United States,
the United Kingdom, Europe and other countries.

ISBN: 978–0–230–34026–8

Library of Congress Cataloging-in-Publication Data

Harris, Jeffrey A., 1955–
    Transformative entrepreneurs : how Walt Disney, Steve Jobs,
  Muhammad Yunus, and other innovators succeeded / by Jeffrey A. Harris.
        p. cm.
    Includes bibliographical references and index.
    ISBN 978–0–230–34026–8 (hardback)
      1. Businesspeople—Case studies. 2. Entrepreneurship—Social
  aspects—Case studies. 3. Technological innovations—Social aspects—
  Case studies. 4. Success in business—Case studies. I. Title.

HC29.H35 2012
658.4'21—dc23   2011031583

A catalogue record of the book is available from the British Library.

Design by Newgen Imaging Systems (P) Ltd., Chennai, India.

First edition: January 2012

10 9 8 7 6 5 4 3 2 1

Printed in the United States of America.

4913 6863 3/12

For Shirley and Merle

CONTENTS

INTRODUCTION

NINETEENTH-CENTURY PHILOSOPHER AND WRITER RALPH WALDO Emerson reputedly said, "Build a better mousetrap and the world will beat a path to your door." It sounds great, but it's not true. Success has rarely been about building the better mousetrap. Commercializing the better mousetrap is the key to success. Inventiveness is important and wonderful, but unless you take that novel idea and make it useful, the multitudes won't seek to find your door. Invention and innovation are not the same. Sometimes they go together, but only the true business titans deliver both invention *and* innovation.

The dictionary defines *invention* as "a new device or process developed from study and experimentation[1]." Nowhere in that definition do you find the words "useful" or "economic" or "solves a problem experienced by many." Only about 10 percent of patents granted in the United States have any meaningful commercial importance that benefits the average citizen, directly or indirectly. Invention is often a precursor of innovation. Over time, innovation may lay the foundation for future invention, providing a powerful regenerative engine for progress in art, politics, business, and technology. Through this building process, wherein invention begets innovation, which begets more invention, which begets more innovation, society and the global economy move ahead. As we have seen over the past one hundred and fifty years, beginning with the Second Industrial Revolution, the rate of change consistently speeds up, compressing the time span between invention and innovation.

History is full of examples of great inventors who died broke and scientists who held numerous patents but never attained volume sales of their products. Alexander Graham Bell exemplifies the classic inventor who was not an innovator. He developed an entirely new form of communication when he patented his "speaking telegraph" in 1876, but he lacked the desire and skill to build a business. Turning the telephone into a practical device also meant having to develop automatic switchboards, install telephone lines, and market the device to enough other people that there was someone to take your call. As Bob Noyce, co-founder of Intel and coinventor of the integrated circuit said, "No businessman would have developed the telephone. It's got to be a maverick—some guy who's been working with the deaf and gets the crazy idea that you could actually send the human voice over a wire....A businessman would have been out taking a market survey, and since it was a nonexistent product he would have proven conclusively that the market for a telephone was zero."[2] Noyce's comment highlights that there are important but separate roles for inventors, innovators, and businessmen, even when they are not wrapped into the same person. Fortunately, Theodore Vail brought the business skills to turn Bell's exciting product into a business by creating American Telephone and Telegraph (AT&T) and the nationwide Bell System.

Thomas Edison was an exception. With nearly 1,100 patents, making him among the largest owners of U.S. patents in history, he said, "I never perfected an invention that I did not think about in terms of the service it might give others....I find out what the world needs, then I proceed to invent."[3] He came to prominence with his inventions of private telegraph machines, stock tickers, moving pictures, the electric chair, the phonograph, and a key breakthrough in amplifying sound waves that made telephones readily usable. Edison understood that the incandescent light bulb would be a mere novelty unless he could find a way to integrate it with an economical and safe electrical distribution system. He found ways to finance his ventures, create the organizations, develop the manufacturing processes, and build businesses around his inventions. Edison invented, installed, and commercialized the dynamos and generators to make and distribute electricity on a grand scale so that consumers and businesses could enjoy the affordable electricity that enables our way of life. Together, Edison's equipment to produce electricity and the devices to use electricity made a formidable combination which ultimately formed the cornerstone of General Electric.

Joseph Schumpeter, the nineteenth-century Austrian-born economist who developed the concepts behind "creative destruction" said that "it was not enough to produce satisfactory soap, it was also necessary to induce people to wash."[4] There has to be a market for a product, service, or invention for it to gain any traction or a meaningful level of acceptance. Without acceptance in the marketplace for products, ideas, and technologies, they linger and die. It isn't that many inventions are not creative or useful to someone. It isn't that most inventions aren't clever. Often, they are. But unless enough people care to employ the invention in a way that makes a big difference in how we live and work, then there isn't much value created. Today, the world is awash in new technologies that overwhelm our ability to use them. Only those technologies that underpin products and services that people want to purchase will gain acceptance, and the rest will be discarded until someone develops the right business model to commercialize them.

Innovation is about commercializing new ideas, new products, new services, and new technologies. We foster innovation in many ways, but there is not a "right way" or a "wrong way." There is no proven cookie-cutter innovation model or secret recipe that all of us can follow. While some people develop a master plan after years of scientific investigation and market studies, and others may have a "eureka moment," most innovation starts from a simple idea which gets modified and adjusted over time as it comes face-to-face with the real world—with competitive responses, shifting regulatory environments, evolving managerial talents, and fluctuating capital markets. We can cite common themes and common denominators, which this book explores, but there is no guaranteed formula for successful innovation, especially innovation that is disruptive. Fortunately, we can learn from many great examples of innovation flowing from those that understood how to make someone else's invention or new idea popular and profitable.

The dictionary defines an *entrepreneur* as "a person who organizes and manages any enterprise, especially a business, usually with considerable initiative and risk."[5] Entrepreneurs are prepared to fail in their attempt to create and implement new businesses, new ideas, new ways of doing things, whether they are for-profit or social ventures, are in start-up companies or large enterprises, and whether they are motivated by wealth or not. Entrepreneurs take risk. They are prepared to be wrong, but they don't expect to be. As Henry Ford once said, "If you think you can, you can. And if you think you can't, you're right."

Harvard's famed business historian Alfred D. Chandler said, "the entrepreneur is an innovator who reshapes patterns of production and distribution by developing new products and processes, by new markets and sources of supply and by devising new forms of organization."[6]

But, not all successful entrepreneurs are great innovators. For example, Bill Gates is among the most accomplished entrepreneurs of all time, but most people would never accuse Microsoft of introducing transformative innovations. After dropping out of Harvard University in 1975, after his sophomore year, to move to Albuquerque, New Mexico, Gates began to build Microsoft into one of the most lucrative businesses ever by pursuing a "fast-follower" strategy and "winner-take-all" execution. We should applaud those achievements but not confuse them with innovation. Similarly, Sir Richard Branson has brought us a wide variety of products and services, ranging from cola to airlines to music publishing to retailing and mobile phone communications to developing his Virgin brand around the world. These have been superb accomplishments reflecting tremendous business skills, but they have hardly been transformative. And, perhaps the most successful entrepreneur of all time, John D. Rockefeller, whose aggressive business tactics in drilling, transporting, and refining oil built The Standard Oil Company into a near monopoly in the United States in the early twentieth century, created a personal net worth exceeding $1 billion at a time when the entire country's GDP was only $90 billion. He did not base his success on invention or new technology; instead it came from an astonishing ability to understand the benefits and power of industrial scale and then devise and implement a strategy to consolidate the fast-growing oil business.

Renowned author and management consultant Peter Drucker said, "Innovation is the specific tool of entrepreneurs, the means by which they exploit change as an opportunity for a different business or a different service."[7] These entrepreneurs/innovators had an instinctive understanding of how to meet the need of customers, often before the customers understand that they have the need. But to achieve commercial success, they had to do more than identify the opportunity. They had to attract outside capital, design and manufacture a cost-effective product or service that could withstand competition, organize and establish distribution channels, build an internal organization, and sometimes, construct manufacturing facilities, all with sufficiently attractive economics to generate and support a sustainable going concern.

Although most successful entrepreneurial enterprises never attain luminary status, many usher in sufficiently powerful innovations to make their mark: Ida Rosenthal and her Maidenform brassiere, improving comfort while accenting women's feminine shape for the

pleasure of all; Michael Dell's customized low-cost personal computers; Baskin & Robbins's choice of thirty-one ice cream flavors—one for
every day of the month; Berry Gordy's hit factory at Motown records;
Jean Neditch's Weight Watchers; Russell Simmons' hip-hop music
genre; Ray Kroc's franchised fast-food hamburgers, french fries, and
golden arches; William Levitt's affordable homes; King Gillette's razor
and disposable razor blades; Jeff Bezos's on-line e-tailer Amazon.com;
and Mark Zuckerberg's Facebook social networking service, and so on.
This is only a sampling from a list that continuously grows, reflecting
the ingenuity, creativity and perseverance of the entrepreneurial class.
Each of these entrepreneurs found a way to deploy their leadership
skills to impact a sector of the economy in a new way, finding a market
segment to exploit and building a sustainable business.

Transformative Entrepreneurs focuses on real innovations and the
entrepreneurs that dramatically impacted the world, often disrupting
existing markets or forging new ones. The intent is not to belittle all
the other efforts that led to "new and improved" but to understand the
conditions and actions that nurtured huge success and a step-function
change in productivity, quality of life, education, transportation,
finance, or entertainment.

The icons in the land of innovation and entrepreneurship created
enterprises that have withstood time, competitive forces, regulatory
changes, generational shifts, and evolving technologies. Most were
inventive people but were not the original creators of the scientific
breakthroughs that formed the cornerstone of their industries. Their
primary skill was not in pioneering but in their ability to improve upon
the original ideas of others, and then put in place the resources to start,
grow, and maintain a business. They had good ideas, well implemented,
but you have to get the plumbing right, which is not easy, and is an
essential contributor to success, especially for businesses that transform
their markets.

Josiah Wedgwood did *not* invent pottery or china, but at a time
when most Brits ate their meals from wood and pewter plates, he recognized that rising incomes in eighteenth-century Britain meant that
many men and women had the money to spend on nonessential goods,
such as china. Taking advantage of socioeconomic changes during the
time of the First Industrial Revolution, Wedgwood built and grew an
international business around high quality products, utilizing new
manufacturing and marketing techniques and thereby creating one

of the world's first brands, Wedgwood China; a brand that stood for high quality, design, and craftsmanship. He decided to develop a high-end image for his products, deploying new techniques such as acquiring aristocratic endorsements, obtaining royal commissions, offering money-back guarantees and free shipping, establishing retail showrooms in London and Bath, and hiring traveling salesmen to sell his wares and open new consumer segments. Wedgwood was an entrepreneur with both creative and commercial skills who had the vision and drive to execute on a pioneering strategy. His company survived and prospered while most of the hundred or so other pottery companies in existence when he started were out of business by 1800.

George Eastman did *not* invent the camera, but he was tremendously inventive. Working tirelessly in the evenings after completing his day job at a local bank in Rochester, New York, Eastman introduced the first mass market camera in the late nineteenth century. At that time cameras were expensive, about $50, and required considerable training and experience to use. Eastman, an accountant by training, sought to bring photography to amateurs by developing a camera that was cheap and easy to operate based on his idea of putting film on a roll. In 1900 he introduced a camera, the Kodak Brownie, which retailed for $1.00, and opened up photography to everyone. The distinctive yellow packaging, the "Kodak" name—which was wholly original—and the company's slogan, "You push the button, we do the rest," were all developed personally by Eastman, who recognized that without creative marketing, the camera alone would not engender success. He was an aggressive user of advertising of all forms. During his lifetime, Eastman left a legacy of philanthropy, donating over $100 million and, endowing the Eastman School of Music at the University of Rochester.

Walt Disney did *not* invent the animated short film, the amusement park, or the television show. However, he was the first to knit them all together, and in the mid-1900s demonstrated the power of creating unique characters and then cross-marketing them through different technologies, media, distribution channels, and merchandizing. The concept seems to have done pretty well and the company's execution remains preeminent.

Steve Jobs did *not* invent the personal computer, the graphical user interface, the digital music player, the computer tablet, or the smartphone. However, Apple has found ways to dramatically enhance the functionality and performance of each of these products and to harmonize them behind sleek industrial design, thereby charging a premium price, while providing thoughtful software and services to assemble a successful business model.

Howard Schultz did *not* invent the coffee shop, nor did Guy Laliberté invent the circus, but Starbucks and Cirque du Soleil both redefined their markets, tossing out the status quo, by creating entirely new types of enterprises on top of well-worn turf that broke away from stagnant business models while introducing their target markets to an entirely novel experience.

Larry Page and Sergey Brin did *not* invent the Internet search engine. Many companies in the late 1990s, including Alta Vista, Excite, HotBot, Infoseek, Lycos, Yahoo!, and others provided Internet users quick and comprehensive access to desired content located on the World Wide Web. However, while completing their Ph.D. work at Stanford University in 1996, Page and Brin developed a novel approach that dramatically improved the quality of Internet search and then began their own company, Google, in 1998 to market this new technology. Google's great commercial success however, stems from a business model that the company "borrowed" from Overture Services, Inc. which tied together advertising placement with search results. However, the combination of Google's superior search technology and aggressive commercialization of the "pay-for-placement" advertising model has propelled it to become one of the most successful companies of all time.

Robert Swanson and Dr. Herb Boyer *did* launch the biotechnology industry. In 1976, this team, consisting of a novice entrepreneur and a University of California, San Francisco professor, each invested $500 of their own money to explore how to create proteins by genetically altering bacteria. Through their new company, Genentech, they took science out of the laboratory and into the commercial realm by introducing a whole new process for creating pharmaceuticals, thereby generating both huge medicinal benefits and profits.

*   *   *

The status quo has never cut it for any business. If an organization, an enterprise or an artist does not move forward, it atrophies. Sometimes it shrivels and falls away very quickly. Sometimes the death spiral takes decades, but the end is almost always the same. Although many people reminisce about the "good old days," in most cases they were not better than today.

Progress is the lifeblood of civilization. Constant evolution, with the occasional non-military revolution, drives societies forward creating a higher standard of living, new art forms, different ways of thinking, and the opportunity to keep life interesting. Sometimes progress is measured in baby steps; and other times, in huge dislocations transform our world: think electricity in the late 1800s, or the Internet in the late 1900s, and perhaps renewable energy in the new millennium.

Even though time frames have compressed over the past twenty years, transformative innovations often take a long time to become obvious. We rarely see it coming until it begins to become part of our normal activities. Sometimes new technology provides the catalyst, but not always. For example, when Fred Smith conceived of the overnight package delivery business in the early 1970s, and then created Federal Express to bring his ideas to fruition, bleeding-edge technology was not the cornerstone of this new service. Similarly, Hugh Hefner's creation of *Playboy* magazine, a publication that sparked a wholesale change in American culture beginning in the 1950s; or James Rouse's real estate developments creating destinations and urban renewal out of tired industrial districts such as Boston's Faneuil Hall, New York City's South Street Seaport, and Baltimore's Inner Harbor; or Muhammad Yunus's Grameen Bank in Bangladesh which ushered in successful and widespread microfinance to help those caught in a perpetual cycle of poverty remind us that clever ideas combined with keen execution behind effective leadership can create meaningful change and value.

When we play historian and look back over the decades, we see the substantial changes that are harder to detect on a day-by-day basis. While this phenomenon of change was once most prevalent in the United States and parts of Western Europe, today it is much broader with the developing countries of Asia, the Middle East and South America participating, and increasingly, positioned to lead the way due to demographic, cultural, and societal reasons.

Each generation offers up creative and entrepreneurial people around the world that have no patience for the way things are. They want to make our lives different, and often better. They are motivated by many forces, with money usually far down the list. These men and women are impulsive, observant, and passionate individuals who want to move the world forward. They do not tend to suffer fools or nonbelievers to their cause. They value results and do not know the definition of failure.

Transformative Entrepreneurs was not written as a scholarly treatise targeting the professorial class, business school researchers or social scientists. Its purpose is to inspire its readers to open their minds, grab some gumption, and boldly support the entrepreneurial ranks. As no one ever wanted a business book to be one hundred pages longer, its message is sweet and succinct. The book draws upon the historical record to support its observations about innovation and entrepreneurship, because there is much to be gained by looking backward as the basis for going forward. As former U.S. President Harry Truman repeatedly reminded his colleagues, "there is nothing new in the world except the history you do not know."[8]

It would be a mistake to study innovation solely from the vantage of the "good idea." To do so unfairly minimizes the stress, strain, and challenges of getting things done on a timely and economic basis using the limited resources that are generally available. Implementation of the good idea through strong managerial leadership, marshaling of scarce resources, persuasive selling, and efficient manufacturing separates out the winners and losers. In a world of constantly changing variables, some macro and others micro, real-time strategy adjustments and powerful commercial execution drive innovation success. The good idea does not stand on its own. And rarely is the good idea born pure, instead it is massaged over time as the marketplace and real-world conditions react. Innovative companies are not solely a function of good ideas, but good ideas tailored for practical use and brought to fruition, usually behind highly committed leadership.

Sometimes commercial creativity comes from new invention or new technology but mostly it comes from an ability to see what the rest of us miss. Dame Anita Roddick, the late founder of The Body Shop, the successful eco-friendly, global retail chain of soaps and cosmetics stores, observed that "there is a fine line between insanity and entrepreneurship ... crazy people see and feel things that others do not." Innovators see opportunity. They do not see hurdles as obstructions, but as challenges to overcome. In fact, for them, striding over the hurdles and besting the challenges is part of the attraction, part of the allure of entrepreneurship, and part of the daily motivation.

Most people are very happy with the status quo. They resist change. They pass up opportunities to try something new or experiment because they might not work. They see all of the reasons why some new product, service, or way of thinking won't be acceptable to even a small fraction of the world. For every optimist there are multiple pessimists. Ted Turner, founder of CNN said, "If you have got an innovative idea and the majority does not pooh-pooh it, then the odds are you haven't got a very good idea."9 We struggle to see the world in a different context than the one that shapes our daily surroundings because we lack the imagination and creative powers to get beyond the here and now, feeling much more comfortable with the glacial pace of evolutionary change. As Henry Ford once said, "If I [had] asked people what they wanted, they would have said faster horses."10

It is challenging for most of us to see the future. History is replete with examples of individuals and corporations that had the golden goose in their hands and let it go, not recognizing the gift that was before them: Western Union turned down its opportunity to buy the Bell patents for the telephone in 1876; General Dynamics could have owned Federal Express, but it passed up its option to buy the struggling company for a pittance in 1973; IBM had the chance to buy the xerography patents behind Xerox Corporation in the early 1940s but did not see a large market opportunity; and the *New York Times* reviewed the introduction of television by RCA's David Sarnoff at the 1939 New York World's Fair and proclaimed that Americans would never sit still to watch it.

Transformative Entrepreneurs looks at people, context, history, and the elements of implementation that move really good ideas into realities. However, to truly appreciate the successes and the challenges of realizing transformative innovations, this book also examines some of the high-profile, highly capable people and companies that tried but failed. Innovation is hard. Most attempts don't work. Without the convergence of the right leadership, market conditions, governmental and societal forces, risk capital, and sometimes, new technology, the probability is high that most attempted innovations will never get very far, and even fewer will rise to a level where the world will pay homage to their creation. And, even when all the pieces do fit together, impassioned entrepreneurs sometimes lose sight of right and wrong, pushing themselves and their companies over the line of propriety and into the realm of illegality.

New business formation does not happen in a vacuum. Government policies and regulations play an important role, either by sweetening an environment that becomes conducive to innovation and entrepreneurial ventures or by making the already nearly insurmountable hurdles even more difficult to get over. As national economies struggle with the impact of globalization, the desire to create jobs and to lift living standards, there is renewed political debate and cultural introspection as leaders try to concoct the winning recipe for spurring increased activity. *Transformative Entrepreneurs* also explores this important contributory facet to better appreciate the magnitude of the challenges that await entrepreneurs around the world.

This book draws attention to a diverse selection of creative entrepreneurs who have made a real difference by transforming our society, significantly advancing our way of life, and generating a step-function improvement in the world. There are numerous examples of people, companies, and enterprises from around the world that illustrate the point that although truly transformative innovation is rare, it happens, and it needs to happen. Hopefully, the reader will begin to see this world through a slightly altered lens.

CHAPTER 1

CHANGING THE LANDSCAPE

Imagination rules the world.
—Napoleon

ENTREPRENEURSHIP OFTEN COMES FROM UNEXPECTED PEOPLE IN unexpected ways. Long resumés of corporate managerial experience and graduate business school degrees do not guarantee success for early-stage companies. Instead, the passion and perseverance of those convinced that their way is best, that their way will work, that their way will win far outweighs sophisticated strategic planning and analysis. There is an artistic nature to successful entrepreneurship. Creative force and individualistic spirit drive innovation in ways that change our world. Few people have the right stuff, but when they do, they can transform industries, economies, and society.

DISCOVERING BY COVERING

If you cloak something, it takes on a different look, as does what surrounds it. Then, when you remove the cover, you see it differently, perhaps with a totally new perspective. The artist Christo and his late wife, Jeanne-Claude, developed an unusual business and an unusual premise for an art form around this simple notion. By shrouding buildings and environs, Christo makes them clearer.

Entering the world at the same hour on the same day in 1935, the Bulgarian-born artist and his French wife collaborated for over fifty years, melding their unique creative vision with a distinctive business model to change the way we look at the world around us. Christo met

Jeanne-Claude in Paris in 1958 when he was commissioned to paint a portrait of her mother. In 1964, they emigrated to the United States where, over the years, they became famous for large-scale projects, such as dropping an orange nylon curtain over a mountain pass in Colorado in 1972; creating a twenty-four-mile-long, eighteen-foot-high "running fence" of heavy white fabric through California's Sonoma and Marin counties in 1976; encircling eleven small islands in Miami's Biscayne Bay with 6.5 million square feet of pink fabric in 1983; and wrapping Paris's famed Pont Neuf, a bridge originally built in 1606, with fabric in 1985.

In 1991 Christo and Jeanne-Claude dotted the landscape north of Los Angeles with 1,660 blue umbrellas, each nearly twenty feet high, while simultaneously opening 1,340 similarly sized bright-yellow umbrellas on the farmland north of Tokyo. The costs for *The Umbrellas, Japan—USA* totaled $26 million, and the project drew approximately 3 million visitors. Permission to wrap the Reichstag in Berlin in over 11 million square feet of silvery fabric and over 50,000 feet of blue rope took twenty-four years to bring to fruition, given all of the governmental red tape involved and the general resistance to the idea. The entire Bundestag debated for seventy minutes on whether to allow the work before a majority voted yes in 1994 so that Christo could spend over $15 million of his own money on the project, which ultimately attracted 5 million visitors. These efforts were a prelude to the culmination of a twenty-six-year effort to place 7,503 sixteen-foot–high "gates" and flowing, saffron-colored fabric panels on the twenty-three miles of walkways of New York City's Central Park in 2005, at a cost of $21 million; that is, it took twenty-six years of persuasion and redesign to accommodate the multiple interest groups and naysayers intent on preventing any change to the status quo. An estimated 4 million people traveled to the park to view the exhibit. Successful entrepreneurs like Christo knock down barriers, refusing to take no for an answer when they believe that their pathway is right.

Christo and Jeanne-Claude would never consider themselves entrepreneurs or businesspeople. In fact, when grouped in those categories they react strongly, as if they were insulted. Their self-image and aspiration floats above the pedestrian view of the commercial animal. Artists are supposed to suffer, and making money, especially a lot of money, seems such a crass notion that can only compromise their integrity and the purity of their work. Nonetheless, Christo's artistic endeavors now generate considerable revenue, which he then reinvests in his next creation. As Christo once said: "I could take the money and buy a castle for Jeanne-Claude, diamonds, a house in East Hampton or a Rolls-Royce. Instead, with that money we build projects."[1]

Christo's imaginative approach strays dramatically from the norm. For most of the past five hundred years Western art has been something that was painted, to hang on a wall, or sculpted, maybe to punctuate a garden. It is meant to have a sense of permanence: the artist and the benefactor expect, desire, and hope that the work will survive for eternity, with luck ending up in a museum or at Sotheby's on auction. Christo's art has always been radically different. Christo never designs his exhibitions to last more than a few weeks. *Wrapped Reichstag* stayed in place only fourteen days. *The Gates* stood in Central Park for only sixteen days. A planned project to suspend translucent fabric panels ten to twenty feet over a six-mile portion of the fast-flowing, winding Arkansas River in Colorado was conceived in 1993, and if and when *Over the River* finally comes to life, it is expected to stay in place for only fourteen days before it is disassembled, and all its material recycled. For Christo and Jeanne-Claude, the temporary nature of their art creates a sense of urgency to see and to become a part of it. If we tally the large crowds that come to view and interact with their various projects, we know that they achieve their goal. The temporal nature of their creations contributes to their allure, but most people also appreciate the uniqueness, the beauty of watching light reflecting off the fabric and its ability to transform the covered structure or surroundings.

Develop an idea for a project – something that does not yet exist. Create the original works of art that detail that idea. Sell these works of art. Bring the project to fruition. Remove the project and recycle the material. The strategy is powerful, but its execution is immensely difficult and certainly not for the faint-hearted. Christo and Jeanne-Claude succeed, like many entrepreneurs, because of the uniqueness of their approach, their immense passion and commitment for excellence, an ability to make things happen, and a long-term orientation.

Christo didn't just sit in his studio with a paint brush, but along with Jeanne-Claude, was out in the countryside or in an urbanscape, in courtrooms, city council hearing rooms, bankers' meeting rooms, lawyers' offices, ranchers' living rooms, fabric manufacturers' factories, and on airplanes flying cross-country and across the oceans and gathering regularly with their engineering team. They are artists who got their hands very dirty attending to the minute details of each project. They wore hard hats and work gloves, carried walkie-talkies, and oversaw temporary workforces of varying size: over three hundred workers were involved in *Pont Neuf Wrapped*; it took 1,880 workers to set up and remove *The Umbrellas* in Japan and California, and more than nine hundred dedicated workers erected *The Gates* and patrolled Central Park during the exhibition. Turning their concepts into reality required military-like logistical skills and precision. All this activity is integral to their art.

SELF-FINANCED

Christo and Jeanne-Claude's moral code required that they not have interference in their work from potential influencers. Accordingly, they funded their projects entirely with their own money. Nor did they accept donations or charge admission fees; they did not sell sponsorships, accept advertising, or cultivate endorsements. They never solicited wealthy patrons to subsidize their efforts. Christo and Jeanne-Claude's projects employed thousands of people to manufacture the necessary raw materials and install their works. They paid lawyers, environmental consultants, engineers, iron workers, and carpenters. They hired surveyors, helicopter pilots, logistics experts, truck drivers, and crane operators. They spent dozens of man-years face-to-face lobbying local landowners, ranchers, farmers, politicians, public-interest groups, and numerous government agencies to gain support for their efforts and to sell their visions. In some years, usually when they were between major projects, their annual revenue from selling Christo's drawings, renderings, and paintings of a planned project was perhaps a few million dollars. But, as large undertakings like *The Umbrellas*, *Wrapped Reichstag*, and *The Gates* came into view and collectors' interest in their work grew, annual sales could exceed $10 million.[2]

Like many successful business models, Christo and Jeanne-Claude's inventive process sounds so simple it makes you wonder why others did not adopt it earlier or copy it for themselves. First, they would develop an idea for a project. Then, over time, Christo would create hundreds of original drawings, collages, lithographs, and scale models that helped him more fully crystallize his vision. Jeanne-Claude sold these works of art to individuals and collectors to generate cash as the two artists began the extremely challenging process of turning their vision into reality. While their projects' complexity were similar to major real estate developments, Christo and Jeanne-Claude's goal was not to accumulate money, but to experience the thrill of completing the project and watching sunlight illuminating and the wind softly ruffling their colored fabric. It is an added bonus if the populace "rediscovers" a landscape or a building that they have temporarily altered.

While Christo and Jeanne-Claude never consciously approached their art as a business, it was, in fact, a business. They had a concept. They created a revenue source. They incurred expenses and considerable upfront capital needs. They personally took a considerable financial risk, often investing their entire net worth in a project.

It was hardly clear in the beginning that their process would work. It was a strategy that had never been implemented before. There were no proof-points. Neither Christo nor Jeanne-Claude had any prior history to suggest that they could do what they intended to do, that they could build a business and a livelihood that was so unique. All their projects met with strong and prolonged objections from local groups and politicians intent on preventing them from attaining their goals. Nonetheless, Christo and Jeanne-Claude created an elite and recognizable brand through the execution of "temporary works of art." Innovation!

Like all transformative entrepreneurs, Christo and Jeanne-Claude changed the landscape; in their case, both figuratively and literally. They created a new way of thinking about art and an entirely new business model to support that strategy. They were classic entrepreneurs, but they do not fit most people's preconceived notion of the greedy, fast-talking, youthful, technology-savvy entrepreneur. They succeeded repeatedly against long odds. They implemented each piece of their strategy numerous times, but always differently, reflecting the needs of the local communities in which they worked and the distinctiveness of the projects. Most impressively, they did not deviate from their principles when pressured to adjust their artistic vision or their economic model. When *The Umbrellas: Japan-USA* suffered from freak wind storms both in Japan and in California, resulting in the tragic death of one of their visitors, Christo and Jeanne-Claude immediately shut down the project.

*   *   *

Christo and Jeanne-Claude sought to reveal by covering. It worked well for them. But there are other ways to get people's attention. Sometimes less subtlety proves more effective. Hugh Hefner's approach to triggering the imagination of his audience was to reveal by uncovering. He wanted to bring his own vision, mores, and personality to an untapped, targeted audience thirsty for the antithesis of family values. He succeeded, and in the process helped usher in a generation of more liberal thought and perspective.

REBEL WITH A CAUSE

The postwar years brought tremendous change to America economically, politically, and culturally. The Cold War was raging. The economy was booming as returning servicemen joined an expanding labor force, making consumer products to meet the needs of a country that had sacrificed for many years. Suburbia was becoming an important sociological force. And, most importantly, there was a population explosion that created the "baby boom." Technology, including the advent of television and availability of affordable consumer appliances, furthered an increase in living standards. General Motors led the creation of a new era of stylized automobiles. On the economic front, disposable income was growing at an annual rate in the high single digits, as the middle class became a large and expanding demographic. Although women had been major participants in the workforce during the war, the standard of living rose in the postwar years, even as women returned to their traditional roles in the home, leaving only one breadwinner in the family. The fashion of the day consisted of the business suit, white shirt, and tie for men (as memorialized in Sloan Wilson's 1955 book, *The Man In The Gray Flannel Suit*), while women wore dresses with hemlines below their knees. It was a time of conservatism. Yet it was also the decade that launched rock 'n' roll (Elvis), beatniks, and the civil rights movement.

In 1956, newsman Mike Wallace interviewed Hugh Hefner on *NightBeat*, his provocative television news show, asking him: "Isn't that really what you are selling here, a kind of high class dirty book?" Hefner responded: "No, there is an important distinction here. Sex will always be an important part of the book because sex is the single thing that men are most interested in ... we don't hide it ... I think that this is a pretty healthy thing." With this attitude and understanding Hefner launched his own powerful business model and unique consumer brand while transforming American society and ultimately proving that sometimes fantasies come true. His entrepreneurial drive coupled with a desire to challenge the status quo reshaped the culture, and his success helped him to establish a personal lifestyle that epitomized his world view. Very few businessmen have ever so successfully embodied their product as Hugh Hefner.

Born in Chicago in 1926, Hefner grew up in a traditional middle-class family. In high school, he demonstrated his first entrepreneurial impulse when he started a small newspaper. After a stint in the U.S. Army toward the end of World War II, Hefner enrolled at the University of Illinois, where, anxious to make up for lost time, he earned his bachelor's degree in two and a half years. He was active on the school newspaper, drawing cartoons, and also edited the campus humor magazine, *Shaft*. In a preview of things to come, Hefner introduced a feature called "Co-Ed of the Month," which profiled an attractive woman on campus and included photographs and descriptions of her activities and hobbies.

In 1948, Alfred C. Kinsey published his groundbreaking report, *Sexual Behavior in the Human Male*, which sold two hundred thousand copies within the first two months of its release.[3] Kinsey and his staff had interviewed several hundred men and discovered patterns of sexual behavior that ran counter to the popular assumptions about American sexual standards and reflected a loosening of sexual mores. Hefner wrote an editorial for *Shaft* highlighting the importance of Kinsey's findings, calling it "perhaps 1948's most important book."

After college, Hefner returned to Chicago, taking a series of jobs without finding much satisfaction in any of them. Hefner's restlessness working for others propelled him into numerous jobs with publishing companies, allowing him to gain an understanding of the overall magazine marketplace while also building a network by getting to know printers, newsstand dealers, and magazine distributors. In fall 1950, despite the added responsibility that came from marrying his college classmate, Hefner felt the entrepreneurial urge and explored the possibility of going into business for himself. He developed an idea for a magazine, which he called *Pulse: The Picture Magazine of Chicago*, and began contacting potential investors, but he was unable to raise sufficient money.

However, finding these jobs unsatisfying Hefner decided to become a college professor. He enrolled in graduate school at Northwestern University in 1950, where he wrote a paper entitled *Sex Behavior and the U.S. Law* that examined the wide array of laws governing American sexual behaviors. In this paper Hefner wrote, "Man's moral life, as long as it does not harm others, is his own business, and should be left to his own discretion."[4]

In 1951, still interested in satisfying his creative urges, Hefner achieved his first publishing success with *That Toddlin' Town: A Rowdy Burlesque of Chicago's Manners and Morals.* The *Chicago Daily Tribune* described it as "a book of cartoons irreverently satirizing Chicago's mores . . . with a collection of drawings that looked like the kind *Esquire* might judge too racy for its picture readers."[5] The cover featured a sketch of a stripper dancing on a table surrounded by smiling men with drinks. The book was a local success, providing media exposure for Hefner on local radio and television shows.

CHALLENGING CONVENTION

Hefner now had the entrepreneurial bug, and in early 1953, he decided to try again to start his own magazine. His concept was simple: create a men's magazine that would reflect his sense of the evolving 1950s generation. At the time, most magazines targeting the male demographic focused on the outdoors. Hefner sought to tap into a different segment of the market, the desired lifestyle of the urban male, understanding, perhaps better than anyone else, that he could achieve success by wrapping a veneer of sophistication around sexual content. Hefner fashioned a winning formula for a magazine that could withstand criticism from a puritanical America. The magazine would promote sexual activity, and tap into men's interest in sex without causing them embarrassment by giving it the guise of respectability. It was a brilliant concept, which he implemented with great tenacity.

To start his new business, Hefner needed a small amount of outside capital. His local bank provided a $600 loan collateralized by the furniture in his apartment. Hefner's father did not like the concept and would not provide any funds, but his mother and brother each gave him $1,000. In total, he raised $8,000 from friends and family as working capital, found a printer and a distributor, and went to work on a card table in his apartment. The original title for his new magazine was *Stag Party,* and it used as its symbol a drawing of a stag with antlers in a smoking jacket standing against a fireplace, brandishing a cigarette holder and a martini glass. Hefner changed the name to *Playboy* after receiving a "cease and desist" letter from a hunting publication called *Stag*. The new title forced Hefner to redesign his logo, and he replaced the stag with a rabbit's head.

To make the magazine distinctive, Hefner resurrected his "Co-Ed of the Month" idea from his college newspaper, creating a feature called "Sweetheart of the Month." In 1949, prior to becoming Hollywood's sexiest starlet, Marilyn Monroe had posed nude for a calendar pin-up. Hefner learned that the John Baumgarth Calendar Company in Chicago owned the rights to the photos but had never published them, being reluctant to send the calendar through the mail because of the U.S. Postal Service (USPS) regulation that forbade sending "obscene material" through the mail. Undaunted, Hefner seized the opportunity by driving out to the company and buying the rights to the Marilyn Monroe photos for $500. Now, he really had something unique.

Using contacts from his days as a circulation manager, Hefner began to promote the first issue of *Playboy*, which would exhibit the famous Marilyn Monroe nude calendar picture, providing enough titillation to line up a national wholesaler for broader distribution. Published in November 1953, the first issue of *Playboy* was only forty-eight pages long and contained a variety of articles about parties, food, office design, sports, and numerous ribald cartoons. Hefner was in business with a totally distinct product targeting adult men who wanted to look at pictures of naked women, but with a touch of class that somehow made it acceptable, if not respectable. With this bold stroke and willingness to challenge the status quo, Hefner positioned himself, and his new magazine, to lead an attack on the nation's view of nudity and sex while crafting a business model with huge market potential. There was never any doubt that sex sells. The challenge had been figuring out how to package sex and nudity in a way that would not be seen as offensive and create a backlash. Not only did Hefner succeed in working out how to do this, but he then pulled together an organization to capitalize on his approach.

The first issue of *Playboy* was the start of an entrepreneurial venture led by an inexperienced founder with limited managerial background, but no lack of initiative or drive. The odds of success clearly were not in Hefner's favor, but the customer response to *Playboy* was phenomenal, with the initial issue selling 54,000 copies—a huge number for a new publication launched on a small budget and no advertising or publicity. He was only twenty-seven years old, but Hef never looked back. The second issue, this time without Marilyn Monroe, but including pictures of other nude women, sold 56,000 copies[6] and introduced the soon-to-be iconic rabbit symbol on its cover. Hefner designed the three-page centerfold featuring one of that month's playmates, who would become known as *Playboy's* Playmate of the Month. Hefner's "entertainment for men" quickly found an audience with the young men about town who enjoyed good, gracious living.

By the end of its first year, *Playboy's* monthly circulation had reached 185,000; that number had risen to 500,000 by the end of 1955, and to 1.1 million copies by the end of 1956, with gross sales totaling $3.5 million and generating pretax profits of $400,000.[7] Hef had created a real business and was also challenging the societal status quo. In October 1954, the magazine applied for the permanent second-class mailing permit typically issued to periodicals (it had been operating with a temporary permit). The USPS denied the application on grounds of obscenity. Exhibiting a trait common to many successful entrepreneurs, Hefner was not going to let the government stand in the way of his mission. Inconvenient rules and regulations were just a hurdle to overcome. Believing that the law was antiquated, he brought a civil action against the USPS in federal court in 1955, challenging its censorship powers, and won.

BRANDING CELEBRITY

With the success of the magazine, Hefner began spending more time at the office. Like many of the most successful entrepreneurs, he was a perfectionist and a workaholic. He was involved in every facet of the publication from the pictures to the stories to the advertising. Nothing went into the magazine that Hefner had not approved. He expected everyone who worked on it to share his passion and belief in what it stood for. Hefner maintained very strict standards for the type of advertising that he would allow into the magazine, turning down products he deemed tawdry. By the late 1950s, Hefner had successfully connected *Playboy* to upscale consumption, and this translated into lucrative advertising contracts with companies selling men's apparel, men's amenities, audio equipment, grooming appliances, jewelry, aftershave and toiletries, credit cards, cameras, liquor, and automobiles.

Playboy encouraged and was encouraged by the growing American consumer society. As Americans' leisure time increased, *Playboy* promoted activities its readers could enjoy in their time off, including jazz, sports, movies, and fiction. As *Playboy* became an increasingly recognizable brand, Hefner implemented a multimedia strategy, moving to merchandise around the *Playboy* logo. In 1959 he hosted the Playboy Jazz Festival in Chicago, which brought together in an outdoor venue the leading artists of the day. *Playboy* made no money from the event, donating its net proceeds to the Chicago Urban League. However, the magazine's involvement with the Jazz Festival upgraded its reputation and helped to improve the image of the magazine so that it began to attract more mainstream advertisers.

In late 1959, Hefner developed a syndicated television show called *Playboy's Penthouse*. The concept was to broadcast a Playboy-style cocktail party, on air, featuring Playmates and top celebrities, white and black. Hefner hosted the show, wearing a tuxedo and smoking a pipe, and mingling with guests that included Ella Fitzgerald, Nat King Cole, Sammy Davis, Jr., Tony Bennett, Sarah Vaughn, Bob Newhart, and Lenny Bruce. The show reinforced the *Playboy* image and lifestyle that Hefner was now living and promoting. Although it was not a huge hit, the show did well in the twelve cities in which it was broadcast and made Hefner a celebrity and an integral part of the Playboy brand. Rarely had an entrepreneur created a business around himself or recreated his public image around his company. He defined the personal brand, but unlike others to come, including Oprah Winfrey, Donald Trump, and Martha Stewart, Hefner was not promoting his name to make himself a brand, but a way of life that would translate into sales for his various media properties.

In early 1960 Hefner took the company's image, as well as his own, to a new level by purchasing an old four-story mansion on Chicago's Gold Coast, several blocks from Lake Michigan. Hef's workday now transitioned into his work night when he renovated the building to include not only personal living quarters but also a venue for hosting large, public parties. The Playboy Mansion generated huge publicity beyond its considerable promotion in the magazine. Hefner, now divorced, lived and worked from the mansion, often wearing silk pajamas throughout the day and night. He became the poster child for the urban male that he targeted in his magazine as he began to live the life his magazine espoused

The creation of the Playboy Club, a high-end, "members only" nightclub in Chicago, featured another invention of Hef's, the Playboy

Bunny; attractive women who served as waitresses and hostesses wearing iconic outfits. The Playboy Club was a huge hit and the company opened many others in cities throughout the country. Then, with a brand name, a youthful image, and riding a rapidly advancing social discourse on sexuality, Hefner continued to build his media empire, adding book publishing and movie production in the early 1970s. Each new media outlet furthered the brand and built magazine circulation. Hefner kept accelerating the growth of his business as he enlarged his market, and an increasing proportion of American society became comfortable with what he was selling. *Playboy* became a vehicle for Hefner to espouse a certain lifestyle, while it also provided him with the livelihood to live that lifestyle.

Playboy continued to break down the puritanical walls, challenging the status quo and often winning. The magazine soon became the sharp edge for political and social issues, including race relations. In 1961, the Playboy Club in Chicago became the first mainstream nightclub to host a black entertainer, the comedian Dick Gregory. Beginning in the early 1960s, "The Playboy Interview" became a regular feature of the magazine, providing an in-depth portrait of celebrities and politicians. In 1962, Hef published the "Playboy Philosophy," his first "manifesto" on social mores, living the good life, and the importance of being an open, tolerant society.

By 1964 annual sales from the magazine had reached $21 million, with Playboy Clubs generating $12 million and other products generating another million dollars. As Playboy Enterprises grew, Hefner began to use the magazine to promote his own liberal ideas. Increasingly, the magazine published articles on politics and broader social issues, reinforcing the rights of the individual and supporting civil rights. In 1966 Playboy Enterprises opened a gambling casino and a Playboy Club in London. London casinos would prove incredibly profitable. As America's involvement in Vietnam was escalating, the sexual revolution was also gaining momentum, and *Playboy* continued to expand, with its monthly circulation topping 5.5 million in 1968. That year *Playboy After Dark* became Hefner's second syndicated television show. Just three years later, in October 1971, Playboy Enterprises had its initial public offering (IPO), selling equity to the public on the same day as Intel. By that time magazine circulation had reached 7 million per month. In addition, there were twenty-three Playboy Clubs, resorts, hotels, and casinos around the world;

a modeling agency; a film business; a record label; and a limousine service. Playboy's ubiquitous bunny logo was among the most recognized symbols in the world.

Now, Hefner was ready for Hollywood. Because of *Playboy After Dark* Hefner was spending an increasing amount of time on the West Coast. Reasoning that if one mansion is good, then two are better, he acquired a huge home in an exclusive enclave of Los Angeles, and began tapping into an even greater number of wannabe starlets and celebrities. The Playboy Mansion West became his new home and headquarters for bacchanalia.

Sensational Achievement

With the huge success of the magazine, *Playboy* had begun to face competition from magazines that published more explicit sexual content, led by *Penthouse* and *Hustler*. The first American issue of *Penthouse*, in September 1969, sold 235,000 copies. Three years later, *Penthouse's* monthly circulation broke 2 million, and by 1976, *Penthouse's* monthly circulation reached nearly 5 million, only slightly behind *Playboy's* 6 million. Other harder core "skin" magazines began to proliferate, pushing the boundaries of sexual content beyond where Hefner could go and still maintain the aura of sophistication that was integral to his strategy and product positioning. These publications were not innovative, and they purposely ignored any sense of upright behavior, seeking to gain a subscriber base by being edgier.

In the 1950s, *Playboy* had pressed hard against the status quo, capturing a previously unserved market. But now, twenty years later, it was part of the mainstream, and other publications were capturing meaningful market share because they were, in some ways, more in tune with the increasingly relaxed sexual tolerance in much of America. An early 1970s survey showed a markedly increased amount of sexual activity since the Kinsey reports. The sexual revolution that *Playboy* had promoted and benefited from was now eclipsing the publication. Hefner had little choice but to move the limit of decorum that he had centered previously on his version of "the bounds of good taste." In addition, Hefner attempted to invigorate the company through numerous organizational and strategy changes, such as launching a Playboy channel on cable television in the early 1980s, but these moves only postponed the inevitable. Once *Playboy* gave up the appearance of respectability, it no longer could masquerade as chic and urbane; it was just another "porn" magazine.

For most of the 1990s and thereafter, Playboy suffered through ups and downs, never regaining the luster of its early years but managing to maintain an audience and a business—just not always profitably. Hefner said, "the magazine is a victim of its own successes. Things it campaigned for—sexual rights, free speech, racial equality—are not what most young men [today] are rushing to read about, if they want to read at all."[8] Sex still sells well, but increasing competition, advancing media technology, and evolving societal norms converged to challenge *Playboy's* role and Hefner's business model. The magazine's monthly circulation fell below 3 million; it continued to lose money, and the company was forced to add more explicit adult content to its cable TV offerings as it tried to retain market position. In late 2010, with an equity market value of only $60 million Hefner, with private equity backers, acquired the company to try to rejuvenate the bunny's withering cache and continue to capitalize on the power of the brand and the bunny logo.

Hefner has lived a life that most men only fantasize about. The frustrated cartoonist from Chicago successfully channeled his entrepreneurial skills and energies to build and maintain a distinctive media business, which, over time, captured an audience and a segment of society. Hefner, the celebrity, introduced a new dynamic by becoming an icon for the urban male lifestyle fueled by the multimedia channels of Playboy Enterprises. But, nothing lasts forever. Eventually social changes and advances in technology, primarily the Internet, made *Playboy* passé, leaving a strong brand name and logo, but not a robust business. However, the fact that the *Playboy* era ended in no way diminishes Hefner's accomplishments as an entrepreneur and marketer. He combined his tremendous skills and foresight with the passion and perseverance that is the hallmark of those who have transformed and disrupted the culture. His efforts first challenged, and ultimately changed, America.

CREATIVITY IS GOOD BUSINESS

Christo and Hefner are not a duo commonly mentioned in the same sentence. But both artists built unique businesses and proved themselves to be very successful entrepreneurs and innovators who reshaped the world around them reflecting their own individualism and philosophies. Neither man had had any formal business training; they picked up their managerial and marketing skills along the way. They both launched their businesses with limited outside investment, which reflected the lack of capital intensity of their operations, but allowed them to pursue their nearly fanatical obsessions to control their final product. Both recognized that whatever was put out into the market was a reflection on them and what they stood for. Despite their differences in style, technique, acumen, and motivation, they shared some important attributes, perhaps none more significant than a singular drive to create something of relevance, a maniacal desire to dictate every aspect of their businesses, and an intense leadership capability and self-confidence that belied their awareness that they might fail. Like many other entrepreneurs that have brought transformative innovation to the market: they had a clever idea, they modified it over time to fit the realities of the marketplace and their evolving vision, they hired a team, and then grew their operations slowly. They were ever mindful of the brand that they wanted and needed to create to sustain the business model that underpinned the fiscal foundation that would allow them to continue and prosper. Both entrepreneurs lived and breathed their businesses: they were a hobby as well as a vocation. They put themselves front and center in the public spotlight to champion their approaches, and each man was proud of his success in reshaping perspective.

Neither of these entrepreneurs were inventors in the classic sense. However, each understood that their creations led to a unique business model, none of which they foresaw at the beginning as part of some master plan with McKinsey-like market studies, or Goldman Sachs-manipulated spreadsheets. For each of them, the business plan proved to be the means to an end, not an end in itself because the business was not much more than a way to finance their goal of forcing us to see through their eyes and feel from their hearts and think through their brains. Christo's objective was (and is) to force us to see the beauty in the world that we so often take for granted in the hectic pace of today's society. Hefner's objective was to wake us up from the hypocrisy he perceived in American society and enjoy life. Once launched, their businesses continued to grow, change, advance and move forward slowly and efficiently knocking down the hurdles that stood in their way, whether it was government regulation or competitive pressures, as each retained control of their endeavor leading the way for their organizations, and in each case forging a brand that reflected the personality, perseverance, and profound passion of the founding entrepreneur.

Christo and Hefner stand out as timeless examples of entrepreneurial success, but distinct in that their imaginations and personal drive created powerful social forces providing the world with a new perspective, shaking off the status quo while constructing a world where fantasies rule.

CHAPTER 2

CREATIVE CONSTRUCTION

Whenever you see a successful business, someone once made a courageous decision.

—Peter Drucker

CREATING A FORMIDABLE, DURABLE ENTERPRISE RARELY HAPPENS because it is extremely hard to achieve. It requires a well-conceived, novel business model and the successful implementation of that model. Getting all the pieces of a business to fit snugly together provides the potential not only for substantial long-term growth, but also for sustainability and unassailability as well. Although Christo's ingenious methodologies will outlive him, his enterprise will not because it centers around his personal skills and perseverance. Hugh Hefner's *Playboy* brand has had an impressive fifty-year run and will likely have legs beyond its founder, though its media properties have entered terminal decline. The most successful, enduring business models become self-reinforcing when management weaves together multiple threads of the enterprise strategy. Companies that have numerous competitive advantages, not solely product advantages, have the potential to become significant, if not dominant, players in their industry and to generate larger profits for longer periods of time. The challenge remains how best to conceive of the innovations that deliver these advantages, and then to execute the winners. Originating a recipe that mixes together the proper ingredients in the optimum amounts is challenging, and infrequently comes prepackaged. Experimentation and multiple iterations are needed before it's possible to winnow out the elements that diminish the end product while also emphasizing those that are most additive; this tends to take time.

Henry Ford's Model T automobile exemplifies a superior product coupled with innovative manufacturing processes that generates huge profit and market share but that ultimately becomes outdated, leaving the company vulnerable to competition. Ford designed his new car to attract a broader market than the traditional early-adopter, luxury toy for the rich. Introduced for $825 in 1909, the Ford Model T sold a remarkable six thousand units in its first year, tapping into a market for the multitude of Americans who wanted an affordable, well-built, reliable automobile. The Model T was easy to drive and simple to repair. As volumes grew, Ford took advantage of manufacturing scale economies, which culminated a few years later in the company's introduction of the moving assembly line for building the car's chassis. Ford had borrowed the assembly line concept from the Chicago meatpacking industry, and it allowed him to meet the growing demand for the Model T, while cutting assembly time from approximately twelve hours per car to only one and a half hours. The greater production efficiencies enabled Ford to lower the price of the car each year while improving its features and functions, creating more value for customers and broadening the market. Ford's famous saying, "Any customer can have a car painted any color he wants, so long as it is black," illustrated the company's determination to lower unit costs. Not only was it less expensive to produce cars that were all the same color, but the "Japan black" paint Ford used also had a faster drying time compared to other paints. By 1921, Ford had manufactured over 5 million Model T's, including 575,000 in that year alone, and held 60 percent of the new car market worldwide. The car's selling price was down to $360, but Ford's profits had reached record levels. In 1927 Ford sold its last Model T, having produced over 15 million units since its initial introduction.[1]

Henry Ford's industrial achievements were remarkable, and his Model T was a great American entrepreneurial success story that democratized automobile ownership, proved the power of scale economies, and popularized the use of the moving assembly line in manufacturing. As one of the preeminent business titans of the early twentieth century, Ford helped to industrialize America and raise its living standards. Although he stood atop his industry for nearly twenty years and his company survives over one hundred years later, the Model T's competitive advantages that had thrust the company into a leadership position could not withstand encroachment from other companies that did not stand still.

Not surprisingly, the market for automobiles evolved over time, and as consumers moved beyond ownership of their first car, they wanted variety in color and design. Ford's business model had become stale, and his resistance to change provided an opportunity for competition to overtake him. Alfred Sloan, the president of General Motors, showed a better understanding of the market and designed a business model for his company to provide "a car for every purse and purpose," complete with an economical manufacturing process that allowed shorter production runs of different vehicles compared to Ford's cookie-cutter approach. In addition, General Motors introduced annual styling changes, and offered customers automotive financing, and value when trading in their current car. Sloan recognized that markets are not homogenous and that for some customers, buying decisions are not solely about product and cost relationship. GM's innovations powered the company past Ford, reminding us that all businesses need to stay dynamic and open to change, especially those that have near-monopoly status.

*   *   *

Henry Ford's single-minded focus on driving down cost propelled his company for many years, but his reluctance to alter his approach and develop other competitive advantages as the market changed around him left his company exposed to Sloan's General Motors. If Henry Ford had stepped back to look at the market more broadly, his company may never have lost the pole position in the automotive industry.

Walt Disney, on the other hand, embraced change throughout his entire career, consistently taking on new risks while also producing an enormous impact on society, selling Midwestern family wholesomeness to numerous generations. Like Ford, Disney was a two-time failed entrepreneur who demonstrated tenacity in the face of adversity. Like Hugh Hefner, Disney mastered the business of selling fantasies. Like Christo, Disney was an artist, but the business model he developed and skillfully executed over time bore little resemblance to Christo's, because Disney's aim was the opposite: he wanted his creative output to endure. His goal was not to do temporal projects, but instead to entice an ongoing flow of moviegoers, television viewers, and theme park patrons who would pay a relatively small amount of money to experience the fantasy world that he created for them again and again.

Boot-strapping the establishment of the modern entertainment conglomerate and milking numerous revenue streams from the simple characters he created, Walt Disney, perhaps more than anyone else in twentieth-century America, created a safe haven for children of all ages to indulge their fantasies. Consistently, Disney proved that his imagination generated its own business magic.

EXPLOITING THE CHILD WITHIN US

Disney pioneered the first modern multimedia corporation whose whole was far greater than the sum of its parts by creatively repackaging his characters from films into comic strips, theme park rides, character merchandise, books, music, educational material, and television shows. He pointed the way for future media companies by showing the huge value-creation potential of leveraging proprietary content and intellectual property across numerous outlets, which translated into higher profitability by lowering development costs and generating higher revenues. The strategy was brilliant, bested only by the implementation. Disney and his team perfected an approach to quality and creativity that had rarely been seen before, driven by his constant attention to detail and dedication to perfection in all of his products.

Like many successful entrepreneurs, Disney was passionate about anything to do with his company, its people, and the creations. He led by example, demanding excellence, inspiring his colleagues, driving hard for perfection and rarely compromising even if it meant added risk, added cost, and time delays. He was prepared to take risks—big risks—and he often put the entire company in jeopardy in pursuit of his vision, but never wavering even when looking over the abyss.

Disney was a believer in the American dream because he lived it. His stories extolled the virtues of hard work, goodness, pursuing one's goals against long odds, and usually concluding with a happy ending. Equally important, Disney reshaped popular American culture by redefining entertainment and leisure time by producing the first animated feature films, and then as an early provider of television programming. Perhaps his most lasting contribution was remaking the concept of the amusement park. Disneyland was a "theme park" that harmoniously exploited the characters and small-town values espoused by Disney's other creations. Disney did not live in the past, though he was a student and purveyor of American history. That he was forward-looking in his imagination of the future is often seen in the storylines of his animated movies and theme park rides, and perhaps most substantially in his creation of the Walt Disney World complex in Orlando, Florida in which he branched well-beyond the entertainment dimensions to create a self-contained city. And, as Walt Disney himself said, "it all started with a mouse."

Disney had no master plan or long-term vision when, in 1922, at age twenty-one, he began his first commercial art business in Kansas City. That was fortunate because the business closed after only one month, forcing the fledgling entrepreneur back to the "employee" ranks, when he began working for a local company producing short animated films. Within a few months Disney had raised a small amount of money with which to launch his second new company, Laugh-O-Gram Films, which specialized in making short films. Alas, this business also folded after a New York film distributor cheated him. Undaunted, Disney headed west to California to make his mark in the growing film business of Hollywood. He started his own studio in his uncle's garage with $500 of borrowed money and began producing short animated cartoons that would run between the feature films exhibited in local movie theaters. Aided by his older brother Roy, and his $250 of savings, they launched Disney Brothers Studio with Walt overseeing the creative side and Roy responsible for certain operational aspects. In 1927 they had their first meaningful commercial success, based on a new character, Oswald the Lucky Rabbit. But, as before, Walt Disney's poor business acumen left him vulnerable to a sharp distributor who maneuvered successfully to get ownership of the character's copyright. Needing a new character, Disney modified the rabbit's appearance and ended up with a mouse, which he named Mortimer. Disney's animated shorts had until this time been silent, but when new technology allowed sound to be added to movies in 1928, Disney Brothers produced the short animated feature *Steamboat Willie,* introducing to the world their talking mouse, renamed Mickey. The Disney Brothers had tapped a rich creative vein that provided the foundation for everything that was to come. Following production of several other Mickey Mouse–based short films, Disney created *The Silly Symphonies,* further taking advantage of the power of the movie soundtrack.

Over the course of his career Disney proved very astute at understanding and utilizing new technologies. As he had done with sound, Disney quickly embraced Technicolor, moving beyond traditional black and white cartoons. In 1932, he won his first Academy Award. Operating on the leading edge of the technology curve carried its own set of risks for anyone in the entertainment industry, especially those with brand names and something to lose. Throughout his long career Disney took advantage of the evolution of cameras, sound, color, and cel generation opportunities to enhance the final product, wow the audience, and set a new baseline for acceptable moviegoer experiences. Disney understood that new technology was his friend, paying large dividends to its early pioneers and devotees, while distancing him from MGM, Paramount, Warner Bros., and other film producers who stuck with the same old formulas and approaches. It was one of the reasons why he purchased exclusive rights to Technicolor's advanced processes for reproducing color on film in the early 1930s.

New characters, such as Donald Duck, Goofy, and Pluto soon added to Disney's stable of popular "stars," especially since each exhibited common human traits and movements, and distinct personalities that audiences easily could relate to. In the first of the synergies that distinguished Walt Disney's company, he understood that Mickey Mouse and his friends would prove to be enticing characters for consumer merchandise. Soon after they had achieved film stardom, Disney charted new ground, opening up another revenue stream that carried minimal incremental cost, by aggressively licensing his characters on a wide variety of products from clocks to clothes to watches to soaps. Disney was well-ahead of his time recognizing that his movies reinforced the Disney brand while serving as a promotional vehicle and enhancing the popularity of the characters. Felix the Cat, a competitive successful animation character that predated Mickey Mouse, had some product licensing, but nowhere to the degree of the Disney characters. Walt Disney's trailblazing approach fortified a spectacular profit generating machine because his cartoon characters never asked for a raise, called in sick, or went on strike demanding a higher percentage of the box office. For Disney, the movie itself was only one component of a broader strategy that created long-term value from his intellectual property.

With television making inroads in America, Walt Disney once again was a pioneer. In 1950, Walt Disney Studios produced the TV special *One Hour in Wonderland*. They followed this success with a regular weekly show hosted by Disney himself titled *Disneyland*. It featured cartoons from the Disney film library and other family fare, such as songs, edits of Disney movies, and miniseries, including *Davy Crockett*, while unabashedly promoting the forthcoming opening of his new Disneyland theme park, allowing the show's viewers to monitor progress of its construction. The television show gave Disney another opportunity to utilize the resources of his studio, and he also recognized that the new medium had the potential to promote all the other creative assets of his enterprise.

In the early 1930s, an enterprising movie theater owner had identified that kids could be an attractive audience for weekend movie time slots. He created a cult following for Disney's mouse on Saturday afternoons, packaging the matinee showing of a feature movie with Mickey Mouse cartoons and giving the children the chance to prove their devotion to Mickey by signing up to be part of a special club, replete with its own pledge of allegiance. Disney greatly expanded this concept of a dedicated club for children when he introduced the television show *The Mickey Mouse Club*, which premiered in 1955, bringing the Disney brand direct to children every day from Disneyland Park. The show quickly became a babysitter for moms anxious for an hour of freedom each afternoon while their children sat still, wearing their Mickey Mouse ears, totally enrapt. Given his extreme attention to detail, Walt Disney approved each member of the young cast ensuring that they had the proper blend of clean-scrubbed look and cheerful attitude. When, smiling and in perfect unison, they sang the show's theme song, spelling out Mickey's name (remember M-I-C-K-E-Y...M-O-U-S-E?), you could almost hear the money flowing into the cash register.

ENCHANTING INNOVATION

Disneyland Park opened in 1955 in Anaheim, California, establishing an oasis for family values and family fun. The project required an upfront investment of approximately $17 million, which was sourced from loans from the Bank of America, the American Broadcasting Company (ABC), and Disney's personal savings, including money he borrowed against his life insurance policy. Most people thought that he was crazy for risking everything to launch his theme park. Only a true entrepreneur would have had the courage to undertake such an unproven, expensive expansion into the unknown. Disneyland Park was an immediate success, attracting 3.6 million visitors in its first year of operation and fashioning another powerful synergistic business element that allowed Disney to make use of his proprietary characters, sell more merchandise, and promote the output of his studio. Unlike the traditional amusement park with its random collection of rides,

Disney and his creative team crafted a more holistic experience, echoing the precepts of its founder: fantasy, futurism, technology, homespun values, American history, and European charm. They tapped into novel technology introducing animatronics to give the theme park characters more lifelike movements. Moreover, Disney's team introduced new standards in cleanliness and efficiency making the park a unique, warm, and welcoming destination for families. The park continued to attract visitors from all over the United States and around the world, becoming a pilgrimage or right of passage for youngsters and their parents.

However, because of lack of funds at the time and the uncertainty of success, Walt Disney was unable to acquire the land around his first theme park. Soon, the streets around the park filled with cheap motels, restaurants, and other tourist traps that degraded the wholesome experience Disney sought to give vacationing families, as well as siphoning off some of his prospective revenues. In the mid-1960s, as the Disneyland Park visitor count continued to increase, Disney understood that he could attract even higher attendance levels if he opened a second theme park on the other side of the country, making it easier for East Coast residents and Europeans to enjoy the unique experience. This time he would ensure that "Disney values" would not be diluted by outside interference. He sought access to a wide swath of land that buffered the visitors from the outside world while also allowing monopoly control of the hotels and restaurants around the theme park. To avoid running up the price of real estate in central Florida, where the Disney team had decided to locate the new park, they purchased land through third-party agents and dummy corporations. But it was not long before the locals figured out that Mickey Mouse was coming to town.

To Disney, doing a repeat of the California Disneyland was not of great interest. Instead, he was motivated by the opportunity to build something more utopian and futuristic. Disney's vision was to build a complete city with full-time residents, schools, retail centers, and office buildings. After more than four years of construction, Walt Disney World opened in 1971 on forty-three square miles of land in the center of Florida—twice the size of Manhattan—putting the city of Orlando on the map. Another of its theme parks, Epcot Center (Experimental Prototype Community of Tomorrow) eventually opened in 1982, helping to realize its founder's initial aspiration. Sadly, Walt Disney never saw his final great creation. He died of lung cancer in 1966, the year before construction began on this Magic Kingdom. Disney biographer, Neil Gabler, captured his accomplishments best:

> He had changed the world. He had created a new art form and then produced several indisputable classics within it...films that, even when they had not found an audience or been profitable on first release, had, as predicted, become profitable upon re-issue....He had built one of the most powerful empires in the entertainment world. And because his films were so popular overseas, he had helped establish American popular culture as the dominant culture in the world.[2]

Walt Disney created a blueprint that would be used by numerous entertainment companies around the world with his innovative approach built on a deep understanding that simple proprietary content can and should be used multiple times in multiple ways. And because Disney had crafted most of his characters with timeless, joyous personalities, his organization was able to continue to embrace and develop them long after he left the stage. In the end, Walt Disney lived the quintessential American entrepreneurial success story. For the benefit of us all, he blended imagination and creativity with doggedness, determination, and drive, so that we can indulge our own fantasies.

*   *   *

Ingvar Kamprad's isn't an American success story, but his creation of IKEA as a leader in global furniture retailing, design, and manufacturing is underpinned by a nearly impregnable business model that is equally impressive and innovative. It was no accident. Whereas Disney recognized that he could use his distinctive characters across multiple distribution channels to build the foundation for huge business success, Kamprad wove together other proprietary ideas to make his company unbeatable around the world.

Growing up in the tiny Swedish town of Agunnaryd, Ingvar Kamprad demonstrated an entrepreneurial flair early in life. As a teenager, in 1943, he became a trader, buying small, inexpensive items in bulk in Stockholm, expanding his product line to include other consumer items, and then selling his goods locally at a markup. He started initially with matches and cigarette lighters, and then expanded his product line to cover other consumer goods that he could bring personally to his customers, such as ballpoint pens and seeds. Kamprad focused on building a business for the long-term, reinvesting his profits and slowly expanding his categories of goods to meet the needs of the local market. As his business grew, Kamprad exercised some creativity, first, by hiring the local milk delivery van to transport goods to his customers, and second, by publishing a catalog, beginning in 1949, so that customers knew what products were available. Although it was far from an obvious move at the time, it was the introduction of furniture to Kamprad's inventory in 1947 that formed the foundation for the IKEA we know today. At age twenty-one, Kamprad had identified a unique market niche in a well-established but relatively uninteresting sector. Within a few years Kamprad discontinued all his other product lines recognizing that by focusing on furniture he could take advantage of Sweden's elevating standard of living and increasing urbanization. His value proposition was simple: sell nicely designed, good quality, affordable furniture targeted at the masses who, increasingly, wanted to move away from the classical heavy, dark-colored, European-style to a more contemporary décor. But, identifying an attractive target market explains only a small portion of IKEA's long-term success. Kamprad set the stage for his company's global success by implementing a comprehensive customer shopping experience, a backend manufacturing and logistics infrastructure, and a unique organization culture that transcended his product offering of contemporary Scandinavian design, constructing a unique, hard-to-replicate business model.

THE POWER OF CUSTOMER SELF-SERVICE

When the milk delivery van changed its daily route, no longer passing by Kamprad's farm, he decided to open his own store, converting an unused warehouse in nearby Almhult into a showroom in 1953. Sales boomed in part because customers got the opportunity to see and touch the furniture before they bought it, something that was not possible with a catalog purchase, which allowed them to appreciate the quality they were getting for the price they paid. In addition, they could get their furniture much more quickly by ordering it in the store. As with Henry Ford's Model-T, increased volume enabled Kamprad to reduce his unit costs. He passed along these savings to customers by lowering prices.

Kamprad recognized very early the huge cost benefits to a retailer of customer self-service. By turning the customer into an active participant, not only in selecting the goods that they want to buy but also in transporting and assembling them, he forever changed the shape of furniture retailing. Perhaps IKEA's most important innovation was doing away with the bulkiness of pre-assembled furniture through the introduction in 1956 of "flat packaging", where all of the components of a piece of furniture lie disassembled in a simple cardboard box. This "flat pack" allowed the company to reduce its shipping costs and inventory space, and it helped to minimize damage during shipping. It also made it easier for customers to get their goods home by themselves, thereby saving time and the cost of store delivery. The flat pack concept developed out of necessity when one of Kamprad's colleagues could not load a table into his car and had to take off the legs so that it would fit neatly into the trunk.

A second pillar of the strategy took advantage of the growing importance of the family car. Kamprad started locating his stores—they now measure 300,000 square feet—outside city centers, where he could access large space more cheaply and also provide customer parking. By attracting customers shopping with their cars, instead of on foot, Kamprad now had access to a low-cost "delivery vehicle" available to transport customers' purchases home. IKEA draws customers into its stores through a combination of clever advertising and the world's largest annual print runs: it now distributes nearly 200 million catalogs of its merchandise each year.

Inside their superstores, IKEA offered a huge selection of products—growing to approximately 7,000 different items—clearly labeled merchandise, and plenty of reasons for the shopper to stay in the store, including child care services, a Swedish café offering Swedish meatballs, and friendly employees. Another pillar was sourcing specifically designed products wherever in the world IKEA could get them made to its standards at low cost. Kamprad always insisted on accessing end product from carefully chosen manufacturers, who had been screened by the company's buying personnel, to ensure quality, cost, factory capacity, and on-time shipments. Today, with over 1,300 vendors, spread across more than fifty countries, IKEA has developed an impressive supply chain that is virtually impossible for others to replicate. Moreover, as IKEA has become such a large customer for each of its suppliers it has tilted the bargaining leverage in its favor to help maintain cost pressure and quality service. This sourcing strategy has the added benefit of putting the capital and management burden on the supplier; IKEA does not have to tie up its own money or staff in manufacturing facilities.

With quality store locations, a wonderful shopping experience, affordable merchandise, IKEA's next strategic pillar was product design that worked all over the world, though clearly emanating from a Scandinavian base. Because IKEA sells only its own designs, customers have a hard time comparing its products to those sold in other furniture stores, avoiding price comparisons. Further, the products, known for their bright colors and high functionality, fit together in a comprehensive decor so that customers can outfit a complete room in their home. Today, they can even buy a home from IKEA.

Passionate about improving efficiency and conserving resources Kamprad invokes cost-consciousness throughout the organization and he leads by example. Part of the cult quality of the IKEA work force stems from their founder's legendary spartan lifestyle despite his standing as one of the world's richest citizens, flying coach class, taking the bus, staying at modest hotels, washing out and reusing plastic cups, and consistently reminding his workers that part of what IKEA sells is "thrift."

Kamprad once said, "retail is detail." He was well-known for his obsessive attention to the smallest part of the shoppers' experience, the company's purchasing decisions, and the employees' needs. His evangelical leadership manifest itself through frequent store visits where he personally shook hands and spoke with every employee creating a bond while further instilling legacy. All of these forces knitted together the strong image and reinforcing practices of IKEA as the price leader and the innovator that tailored a "cash-and-carry" business model to furniture retailing. As with Disney, each of IKEA's strategic strands works together ensuring the company's success while maintaining high margins and even higher entry barriers.

IKEA opens only a few new stores each year to maintain control, ensure retail location discipline, and not overtax the supply chain. It has proved to be a winning strategy. With operating margins ranging from 10 to 15 percent per year on $33 billion of retail sales from over three hundred stores in thirty-eight countries, IKEA has become one of the largest and most profitable private companies in the world, and it was financed entirely from the founder's personal savings and retained earnings.

Kamprad did not start his company with a well-crafted business plan that outlined how he would get into furniture retailing. He started his business in one direction but then saw an opportunity, pivoted to take advantage of it in response to demand, and then, slowly, taking very small steps he created a company which consistently found ways to beat back competition while forging new ground around the world. Innovations around the flat pack, customer self-service, and proprietary furniture design available only in their huge stores allowed IKEA to create a distinct and total customer buying experience. Growth was measured, and remains measured allowing the organization and its suppliers to keep pace so that everything stays under control and mistakes are minimized. IKEA's business formula is well-understood today, but it is so hard to replicate, and for others to meet its selling proposition, they have to match it in its entirety from product design, product selection, sourcing, cost, company culture, and now brand image; a very tall order.

*   *   *

Walt Disney exported pure Americana through his animated characters, movies, and theme parks, and Ingvar Kamprad exported a taste of Scandinavia in every IKEA store and piece of furniture. Both entrepreneurs showed that meticulous attention to detail and a determined, yet steady approach to building one's business without deviating from the founders' core values can lead to overwhelming success on an international scale. Most importantly, both men wove together unique ideas into innovative business models and then built the organizations to drive sustained profitability. Their innovations furthered the distinctiveness of their companies and created huge entry barriers for potential competitors.

Whereas Walt Disney packaged three dimensions of fantasy and served them up so appealingly that he captured the imagination of the world's children and their parents, Ingvar Kamprad attracted families and young couples to his stores and then kept them there, shopping for as long as possible. Both Disney and Kamprad understood that creating proprietary products and then offering them to their target consumers in a fresh, appealing, and comprehensive manner made for a successful sustainable business.

CHAPTER 3

TRUE GRIT

Only those who are prepared to fail miserably can achieve greatly.
—Robert F. Kennedy

HORATIO ALGER, JR. STORIES OF THE LATE NINETEENTH-CENTURY tell of city boys who came from poverty and successfully rose to create significant personal wealth through honest hard work, courage, and integrity, going "from rags to riches." It is a popular notion that this opportunity is available to anyone in America, and numerous examples point to such success, including many discussed in this book. Like Christo, Disney, and Hefner, most entrepreneurs come from humble backgrounds and have little to lose if their ventures fail. But, what if you have a lot to lose? What if you come from a well-to-do family and do not have to work hard, take risks, or develop new ideas in order to prosper? Would you wager your birthright on the chance to turn your dream into reality?

Some people argue that those who come from wealthy families have significant advantages in the entrepreneurial world because they attended "good schools," formed social and business networks with others that have a greater chance of prominence, know how to access the funds to start and grow a new enterprise, including from their friends and families, and often have had strong, successful role models to emulate. It is a compelling argument, but it misses two essential elements: risk tolerance and native ability.

In fact, having something to lose often makes people more risk averse. Entering the world with the proverbial silver spoon in the mouth usually dictates a career path that is long on safety and short on willingness to lose one's social status, hefty bank account, or country club friends. For some wealthy people, these forces magnify the downside risks of starting a new business, although for others, conversely, they provide added motivation and enticement, with an improved understanding of the accolades that come from success. Entrepreneurship is, in part, about evaluating risk and calibrating opportunity. Assessing both the upside and the downside comes with the territory. However, if you have something to lose, your downside is greater than that of Horatio Alger's street urchins.

Despite this added imbalance, some wealthy people further demonstrate their boldness by putting it all on the line. For them, the powerful attraction of building something, of proving to themselves or their parents or their peers that their place in the world stems from personal smarts, gumption, and skills dwarfs the fear of failure or cruising through life concerned that they are perceived solely as freeloaders, trust fund babies, lucky sperm club members, or raw inheritors. They have much to lose, but sometimes they win. Sometimes they win big.

*   *   *

Fred Smith's father died when he was only four years old, leaving him a large inheritance built up from his entrepreneurial activities: a passenger bus line and one of the first short-order restaurants, The Toddle House. Born in Mississippi in 1944, Smith grew up in privilege. The trust fund that his father left to be shared with his two stepsisters totaled a sizable $14 million. Matriculating at Yale University in 1962, Smith encountered New England society, counting among his schoolmates George W. Bush and John Kerry. After graduation Smith enlisted in the U.S. Marine Corps. He shipped off to Vietnam as a platoon leader and flew over two hundred missions during the war. When he was discharged in 1969, Captain Smith brought home a Silver Star, a Bronze Star, and two Purple Hearts. Smith wasted little time going into business after returning to the United States, immediately using $750,000 of his inheritance to buy an aviation maintenance company based in Little Rock, Arkansas. He grew the company quickly and added an aircraft brokerage capacity. Annual revenues reached $9 million after his second year. But Smith had bigger ideas and decided to implement them.

While at Yale Smith had written a paper in one of his economics classes about increasing computerization of the business world and how it would likely force changes in the economy. Smith understood that as enterprises began replacing people with complex equipment, they would demand that those machines function all the time. Smith's idea was a novel distribution system for the rapid delivery of spare parts to minimize the downtime of expensive machines, such as aircraft and office automation equipment. Smith's goal was easy to describe. Figuring out how to design and implement a state-of-the-art nation-wide logistics system proved much more complicated.

GIANT STEPS

Smith's objective was to make sure important and valuable goods could be delivered quickly to wherever they were needed. He concluded that the best way to accomplish this was to put in place a large network of airplanes and delivery trucks around the country so that suppliers could ship from anywhere to anywhere almost instantly. Smith's idea was to have his company collect packages during the day, and then fly them each evening to a central spot where they would be sorted and reloaded onto planes that would take them to their final destination, where a fleet of trucks would carry them to the intended recipients the next day. A similar concept had been used in the financial services industry, where the documents needed in a specific transaction would be collected and worked on in one locale and then delivered by messengers the following day for clients to sign. To make his idea work, Smith would need airplanes that were not expensive, could carry a reasonable amount of cargo, and that flew fast. Fortunately, Dassault had introduced the Falcon 20, a new ten-passenger business airplane that fit these requirements. Next, Smith had to figure out a routing system so that planes did not spend too much time in the air or on the ground. He designed a network around a new topography based on a hub and spoke system that minimized the time it took for packages to be collected from senders and delivered to recipients.

Most entrepreneurs start their businesses small so that they can test their ideas, hone them over time, and then build up resources and experience before they expand. Smith's vision and network design did not afford this luxury. He had to have a critical mass of planes, trucks, employees, and customers to make it all work. Smith had determined that he would have to launch his service to a minimum of twenty cities spread throughout the country to develop enough traffic to support his operations. This would take considerable upfront investment and the patience to endure an extended period of losses while proving the business concept, an approach well outside the norm of most start-up companies. Not only would Smith need lots of money, he would also need to put in place an organization prepared to join him in taking the risk, and then he would need information systems to track the packages, planes, trucks, and people so that the company could provide the required level of customer service.

Starting any new venture carries numerous challenges. Starting a new venture that requires scale at the outset runs counter to most accepted business practice. Smith was only twenty-seven years old and had only limited real-world work experience. However, having spent several years overseeing the hundreds of soldiers under his command in Vietnam, he was undaunted. He saw a large market opportunity and ran toward it, recognizing that if he could overcome the challenges, the winnings would be great.

Since the 1800s the U.S. Post Office (USPS) had been responsible for moving the vast majority of mail and packages throughout the country. Its reputation was extremely poor because of its slow and inconsistent service. However, it operated under a regulatory monopoly for many types of mail, allowing only a few companies to establish operations for selected niches of the market. For example, Railway Express and United Parcel Service (UPS) expedited delivery of packages using the existing rail and trucking infrastructure. In 1953, UPS also began employing unused cargo capacity on passenger airlines to provide two-day freight service to the east and west coasts.

Moving freight around the United States was a huge operation when Fred Smith decided to launch his new company. Approximately 1.5 billion tons of freight shipped annually in the United States, but because of the hefty expense involved, only the most valuable and time-sensitive cargo, less than 2 percent, went by air. The industry was highly fragmented. Hundreds of local trucking companies acting as freight forwarders had captured most of the business because they had the customer relationships and equipment to pick up and deliver packages in coordination with the passenger airlines and the USPS. Emery Air Freight was the largest freight forwarder. Also, Air Cargo, Inc., a joint venture of twenty-six different airlines, owned a trucking business that provided delivery services at many airports around the country.

Through 1978 only the USPS was authorized to deliver documents. But customers, frustrated by the poor service and high prices, were demanding alternatives. Smith lobbied Congress for changes in the regulations, successfully promoting amendments to the long-standing Private Express Statutes Act, allowing private carriers to transport certain types of publications and documents as long as they were delivered overnight at prices at least double the post office rates. If, as Smith prophesized, companies would pay extra for faster and more dependable delivery of their time-sensitive documents and spare parts, he would have the foundation for an attractive business.

The air freight business differs substantially from the passenger airline business. First, freight can be flown at night when the airports and skies are less crowded. Second, there is little need to offer more than one flight per day because most businesses don't need multiple deliveries during normal working hours. Third, the collection and delivery of cargo, packages, or documents offers significant economies of scale, since vehicles need to travel shorter distances between pickup and delivery points as the density of shipments increases. However, freight requires more ground handling than do airline passengers, who get themselves to and from the airport. It also suffers from diseconomies of scale due to the complexity of the sorting process, which increases with the number of delivery spokes.

Every day the Federal Reserve System moved millions of canceled checks between commercial banks. Smith decided that the government agency would be the perfect customer for his new company, and in May 1971 he succeeded in getting an audience with administrators of the Kansas City branch of the Federal Reserve to pitch them on the idea of overnight air delivery as a way to reduce the time required to clear checks. Before getting their response to his proposal, Smith went ahead and formally incorporated his new company, calling it Federal Express, in part to help woo this potential customer. He financed the company's early operation with $500,000 split between his personal funds and the family trust. Feeling confident about gaining a contract, Federal Express bought two Falcon 20 jets for $3.6 million with additional funds borrowed from a local bank and guaranteed by the family trust, with the planes serving as collateral. In August 1971, the Federal Reserve rejected Smith's proposal, leaving his newly-formed company with two beautiful airplanes, $3.6 million in debt, no customers, and no capital with which to launch the business.

DOGGED PERSISTENCE

Like all tenacious entrepreneurs, Smith was undeterred. He formulated a plan to raise additional funds and hired two consulting companies to size the potential market for Federal Express's services, recognizing that he would need outside corroboration of the company's potential to attract large investors. Both market studies concluded that Federal Express had a big market potential, though to break even, it would need to move 11 percent of the country's 20.4 million annual shipments of packages weighing under fifty pounds. The consultants estimated that it would take the company three years of full-scale operations and an additional $16 million of capital to reach this milestone. Nonetheless, the lead consultants from each firm became so excited by the Federal Express opportunity that they joined the company in senior management roles.

In addition, Smith had to modify the Falcon 20 jets, which had been designed and built to carry passengers, not to move cargo.. He also had to secure waivers from the federal government allowing him to use the planes because they were too heavy to be classified for "air taxi service." This would have layered significant additional regulatory bureaucracy on the company. Smith went to Washington D.C. to personally lobby Congress to get the regulations changed, succeeding in July 1972.

Fred Smith continued to have big dreams. To reach scale, Federal Express would have to operate many more than two airplanes. In July 1972, the company purchased eight used Falcons with $16 million in loans, including one that Smith personally guaranteed. Now having sufficient airplanes to demonstrate a basic delivery capability, Federal Express undercut all other bidders and finally won its first contract. It would move mail on the weekends for the USPS for $300,000 per month. Federal Express was ready to fly.

Initially, Federal Express located its headquarters in Little Rock, Arkansas. Smith and his team recognized, however, that this was not an ideal location for the primary sorting hub or for optimizing the flying time of its fleet. In determining the best place for its operations, Federal Express had to minimize the potential impact of both winter weather and summer thunderstorms, while also accessing an airport with sufficient runways and state-of-the-art landing instrumentation.

Fred Smith had high expectations for the growth of his company, so he wanted to place his operations where there would be an abundance of relatively low-cost, nonunion labor. Federal Express found it could meet all of its needs in Memphis, Tennessee, and when the municipality offered to float a twenty-year general revenue bond to finance the new sorting facility, which would bring much-needed jobs to town, the company had its new headquarters location.

The nature of the service Smith wanted to provide required a substantial infrastructure with a heavy upfront fixed-cost structure before there could be any meaningful business. To give his approach a chance to succeed Federal Express would expend meaningful capital, well in excess of what his personal family assets could provide, putting Smith's fund-raising prowess to the test. In quest of an incremental $20 million of debt and equity financing in February 1973, Smith sought the assistance of a venerable investment bank, White Weld & Company. Before taking on the assignment White Weld required that Smith personally invest $2 million, which he did via a loan from the Union National Bank in Little Rock collateralized by the family trust. Concerned that his sisters would not want more of their inheritance tied up in his risky venture Smith chose not to discuss it with them and allegedly prepared and signed minutes of a trust board meeting authorizing the guarantee without their permission.

For the formal launch of Federal Express's package delivery service in March 1973 the company had put in place operations to support the pick-up of packages in five cities with delivery to nine cities across the United States. In addition, it put together a marketing and sales plan to attract initial customers, formulated a price list, bought delivery trucks and hired drivers, recruited new employees to sort the expected volume of packages in Memphis, and set up integrated information and financial systems to track each package and manage the accounts. Management had projected that on its opening day of business Federal Express would transport between three hundred and four hundred packages. Instead, the first day's volume totaled only six packages, so the company deferred the official start-up of its aircraft fleet and used commercial airlines to transport the packages directly to the intended destinations.

To make commercial sense Federal Express had to provide services to and from enough cities to attract a sufficient level of customers. However, to operate in more cities required more planes, more people, more trucks, and more capital; much more capital. Until it could raise the necessary funds Federal Express continued to use the passenger airlines to move its packages, because that remained the most cost-effective approach, even though it had paid to acquire all of its own aircraft. In April 1973 Fred Smith went out to raise more money. He was introduced to Charlie Lea, a pioneer in U.S. venture capital, whose firm, New Court Securities, managed $75 million of Rothschild family money. In the early 1970s very few venture capital firms existed and most had not been around long enough to enjoy much success from start-up companies. After reviewing the opportunity, New Court decided against investing in Federal Express. The firm understood that once the company's operations reached critical mass, the marginal profit of the incremental package would be wonderful, but it concluded that Federal Express was too risky because of the potential for it to experience large losses before it generated enough volume to become profitable. Nonetheless, Fred Smith pushed ahead, continuing to hone the company's operations, including having his planes move empty boxes around the country to ensure that the company could provide a high level of service. On the day it finally went live—twenty-two months and $25 million of financing from the date of the company's incorporation—Federal Express moved one hundred and eighty-five packages into and out of its Memphis hub, serving twenty-five cities. It was a start.

However, money, or the lack thereof, continued to cloud the company's future. Suppliers got nervous about providing various goods and services fearing that they would not get paid. One pilot had to use his personal credit card to pay delinquent landing fees and a truck driver traded his watch to buy fuel for his delivery van. Then, in May 1973, with the company on the brink of bankruptcy, Fred Smith convinced General Dynamics to guarantee a $23.7 million loan from the Chase Manhattan Bank in exchange for a four-month option to buy 80 percent of his company for only $16 million. Federal Express used these funds to acquire more aircraft to support operations to and from additional cities. However, General Dynamics let its purchase option lapse, never acting on the opportunity to own Federal Express. In July 1973, on the way home from a failed fund-raising trip, Smith detoured to Las Vegas where he hit the gaming tables and turned a few hundred dollars into $27,000 before returning to Memphis in time to pay delinquent fuel bills.

Federal Express was operating on the ragged edge, teetering from a lack of funds while slowly proving its concept. When daily package volume reached one thousand by the middle of 1973, Charlie Lea changed his mind and decided to invest agreeing to lead a funding round to attract money from other venture capital firms. Smith had already invested $2.5 million of his own money in the company, plus $5.4 million from his family trust. By November 1973, Federal Express raised $24.5 million of new equity and $27.5 million in new loans. It wasn't enough.

Despite all of the headwinds buffeting Federal Express in its early days, a further monumental test of the management team and the underlying business concept arose in late 1973. In response to U.S. government actions in support of Israel during the Yom Kippur War, several Middle East countries retaliated by staging an oil embargo. The action by the Organization of the Petroleum Exporting Countries (OPEC) had a nearly cataclysmic effect on Federal Express, plunging the United States into recession and increasing jet fuel prices fivefold. Still, by the end of 1973 Federal Express was delivering 3,000 pieces each day.

Federal Express was ramping up its operations and expected to use four million gallons of jet fuel in 1974. However, in January, Congress enacted the Emergency Petroleum Allocation Act rationing jet fuel in accordance with the airlines' 1972 usage levels. The new regulation would mean that Federal Express was only entitled to 1 million gallons of fuel. As before, Fred Smith traveled to Washington to try to convince Congressmen and regulators that his company deserved more than that. He got the 4 million gallons of jet fuel he needed.

Despite the bear market on Wall Street and the deepening recession, Federal Express continued to ramp up its daily volume. Revenue increased but losses still totaled about $1 million per month prompting Fred Smith to go out and raise even more money. The good news for him was that the positive trend in his business counterbalanced the tough economic environment, allowing the company to raise incremental debt and two new rounds of equity financing. In each equity financing round Federal Express was forced to sell its shares at lower prices to venture capitalists who remained wary of investing in a company that had not yet shown profits. However, by the end of 1974, daily package volume reached 10,000 pieces, and Federal Express was growing 20 percent per quarter.

At the request of Smith's sisters, the FBI began investigating the family trust commitment that Smith had falsified several years earlier. The poor results of the business and Smith's unethical behavior created considerable family tension. In January 1975 Smith was indicted by a grand jury for forging documents and violating his fiduciary duties as a trustee of the family trust, but was acquitted at the end of the year and subsequently settled with his sisters out of court.

Revenue finally surpassed the large fixed costs of airplanes, trucks, people, and equipment inherent in Federal Express's business model, and the company generated its first profit in late 1975. With the business gaining momentum, Federal Express began a series of iconic television advertising campaigns to further highlight the quality and reliability of its overnight delivery services.[1] The next year Federal Express grew to 2,000 employees, and the company was operating thirty-two Falcons, nine other aircraft, five hundred delivery vehicles rented from Hertz, and was delivering an average of 19,000 packages per day to seventy-five cities. By the time of its IPO in May 1978, Federal Express had attracted more venture capital than any other company in history, eating up $91 million of start-up equity prior to turning profitable. Fred Smith had pulled off one of the most remarkable new company challenges ever and in the process created an enduring company that has profoundly changed the way the world does business. By his own admission, the entire notion of trying to start a company at that time with such large upfront capital requirements, its need to get the government to change its regulations, and a business model that necessitated a broad base of cities for success was foolhardy. But as Smith said in an interview in 1998, "I was willing to take a chance, because losing wasn't the worst thing in the world that could happen to you. I had seen that very clearly [in Vietnam]."[2]

* * *

Successful entrepreneurs take chances. They believe in themselves and their ideas probably more than their backgrounds and experiences would suggest reasonable. But, once they get focused on something their resolve and determination come through. They show an unusual resourcefulness and creativity when solving problems. They demonstrate a desire to win. Fred Smith had that desire. So did Ted Turner.

Ted Turner once said, "If I had any humility, I would be perfect." Ted Turner is not perfect, but his ability to create new, profitable enterprises often risking everything he owned to try to build something even greater places him in truly distinct company. Turner had the courage of his convictions, more than once transforming his business by gambling all. Fred Smith inherited sufficient wealth from his father and could have lived well without ever taking the risk of starting Federal Express. But that did not stop him. Ted Turner inherited a multimillion dollar billboard business, Turner Outdoor Advertising, when his father committed suicide in 1963. At the time Turner was only twenty-four and the family business was in debt despite having a leading share of the billboard business in the southeastern United States. To help the company survive, Turner's father had sold the Atlanta, Georgia, division shortly before putting a gun in his mouth and pulling the trigger. His son had different ideas about the future potential of the Atlanta market believing that it could be a profitable contributor to the family business. Through very tough actions, including threatening to put new billboards in front of those that had been sold, and hiring some of the former employees, Turner succeeded in buying back the Atlanta division for $200,000 worth of company stock.

EGOMEDIA EXCELLENCE

Over the ensuing years Turner successfully built his media business, getting what he wanted by being both ruthless and creative. He made his investment decisions based on gut instinct and then drove himself and everyone around him to new heights of achievement to attain his desired goal. Billboards provided steady cash flow underpinning Turner's desire to own a more substantial media business. In 1968, now bored by the billboard business, Turner branched out into radio broadcasting, buying several radio stations throughout the south, including some that were in need of resuscitation. In 1969 Turner took the next step by buying into television broadcasting. His first quest was a UHF[3] station in Atlanta, Channel 17—which still broadcast in black and white, not color—an unheralded, antiquated, money-losing local station that had a small viewership, poor facilities, limited programming, a weak broadcast signal, and no great reason for continued existence. Turner's friends and business advisors counseled him not to divert the positive cash flow from billboards and radio to subsidize the television station's $500,000 annual loss. But Turner was undeterred. Excited about the future of television broadcasting, he bought the station for $2.5 million in the stock of his company. However, Turner understood that, as with billboards and radio, the success of a television station comes from selling advertising. Turner knew how to sell. He could dial up the charm, offering impassioned arguments to attract new advertisers. Like Walt Disney and Hugh Hefner, he also knew how to exploit one communications medium to support another. He used his unsold billboard space in Atlanta to advertise his new television station. To increase viewership, Turner captured network programming from NBC that was not running on the local NBC affiliate because it had other priorities in certain time slots. While other Atlanta stations broadcast news and religious programs, Channel 17 offered old movies and reruns of sitcoms. Within a few years, the station was making money and soon started generating big profits. Turner had bet his company and won.

In 1972, Channel 17 bought the broadcast rights to sixty games per year of Atlanta's major league baseball team, the Atlanta Braves, immediately boosting viewership. Then, in 1976, he purchased the team, putting down a small amount of cash and agreeing to pay the rest of the purchase price over ten years. This made Turner among the first baseball team owners to also control his own television station and to take advantage of the fit between the two businesses. As owner, he now had the broadcast rights to all one hundred and sixty-two of the Braves' games. This enabled him to fill air time with an enormous quantity of original programming that would have been extremely expensive to duplicate through old movie and sitcom rights.

If owning and broadcasting the baseball team was good, then duplicating the strategy with the local basketball team, the Atlanta Hawks, was even better. Not surprisingly, that is exactly what Turner did. By the mid-1970s Turner Communications, as the business was then called, a combined media company offering of television, radio, and billboards was gushing cash in time for its leader to seek another new challenge. The new broadcast trend was satellite communication, point-to-multipoint, beaming a television signal up to a satellite transponder that could then send it back out and across a wide geographic footprint. Satellite distribution of video signals provided a meaningful improvement over microwave and telephone line for those who wanted to disseminate their programming to the thousands of independent cable operators that were sprouting up across the United States. HBO became an early pioneer in cable programming, starting a dedicated twenty-four-hour movie channel. Turner wanted to have his own twenty-four-hour channel. Even before receiving government approval or gaining access to scarce transponder space on an orbiting satellite, he began spending money to build his own dedicated transmitter. Like Fred Smith, Turner had to overcome significant regulatory hurdles, and he personally lobbied the U.S. Congress to ensure satellite capacity for his company when network broadcasters sought to stop all satellite broadcasting.

Turner renamed Channel 17 "Superstation WTBS." In an era of limited programming sources, cable operators were grateful to have more programs, and they signed up to access Turner's eclectic lineup of sitcom reruns, Atlanta sports, and old movies. Because cable systems paid only a nominal fee per subscriber for the broadcast signal, they could include the Superstation in their basic subscription packages, which permitted them to offer programming that was not available elsewhere at no additional cost. It became the first advertiser-supported cable television station able to broadcast to all the cable operating systems in the country, allowing national advertisers to tap into this large market more easily.

With a growing media empire, access to more satellite transponder time, and a network of relationships with cable operators throughout the country Turner once again charged forward, looking for new ways to expand. He understood that proprietary programming drove successful cable television channels, but with ESPN targeting sports broadcasting, the networks controlling original programming, and HBO leading with movies, Turner saw "news" as the only large space remaining. Turner modeled his television news concept on the all-news radio stations in New York. No one had ever contemplated twenty-four hours of television news seven days a week. The likely upfront cost, an estimated $50 to $100 million before the breakeven point, seemed overwhelming, and the challenge of accessing video footage of important events from around the globe on a timely basis was even more daunting. Not to Ted Turner.

Turner's prior ventures had given him a deep understanding that satellite technology had leveled the playing field between cable and the three U.S. television networks, ABC, NBC, and CBS, their nationwide affiliates, and overseas news bureaus. However, would anyone watch news all day long in a country conditioned over many years to receiving thirty minutes of summarized national and world news once each evening from trusted anchors such as Walter Cronkite, David Brinkley, Chet Huntley, Harry Reasoner, and Frank Reynolds? Turner did not want his twenty-four-hour news network to simply broadcast stories about local fires, the police blotter, or other mundane content to the national viewership his satellite transponder could access. Without good content there would be no viewers, without viewers there would be no advertising or cable fees, and without advertising revenue, Ted Turner would lose not only his quest for twenty-four-hour news but maybe his entire media empire.

BETTING THE RANCH, AGAIN

Turner proved relentless in his drive to launch CNN – the Cable News Network. He hired numerous television-savvy newspeople, reporters, producers, directors, computer-graphics artists, technicians, and journalists. He bought the latest broadcast equipment and personally sold cable operators around the country on adding his new channel to their existing lineups, while also tapping national advertisers. To help finance his new venture, Turner sold his Charlotte, North Carolina, television station for $23 million in 1980. Most people, including many news and broadcast insiders, thought Turner, once again, had lost his mind and would probably lose his shirt trying to establish a new cable channel devoted solely to news.

His efforts were not without their troubles, however. With ground operations ramping up, the RCA satellite that was to carry CNN's television signal had blown up on lift-off in December 1979. Without a transponder, there would be no CNN, and Ted Turner was not about to watch his venture die before having a chance to see its dawn. He flew to New York to negotiate access to a spare transponder on an existing RCA satellite, trying to preempt potential competition from other stations. He succeeded, and on June 1, 1980, he launched CNN. It was far from an instant success. Turner had not yet signed up many cable operators to take his news feed, and the entrenched network news organizations worked actively to isolate CNN from news stories, video feeds, and pictures. CNN exercised its legal right, and sued the network news organizations to ensure fair play, ultimately prevailing. As with many start-up ventures, the early days were not pretty. Lacking both the households and advertisers to cover its costs, CNN was losing an estimated $2 million monthly. Losses would continue to mount as CNN increased its news-gathering capacity. However, it was impossible to have dedicated CNN film crews and journalists all over the world to capture any and all breaking news stories. Creatively, CNN ameliorated this burden, breaking new ground by becoming a clearinghouse for sharing news among existing broadcast network affiliates who wanted real-time access to stories captured by other tele-vision stations and who were not willing to wait until the prime footage had already aired on the networks' evening news programs. Through this cooperative sharing arrangement, CNN duplicated much of the networks' newsgathering infrastructure at a fraction of the cost pig-gybacking off of the local newsgathering organizations already in place and supported by the local stations.

Slowly, CNN migrated the television news show from being an aggregator and summarizer of the day's events broadcast once each evening to a showcase of real-time, almost participatory news, view-ing with an immediacy that the network news shows could not match. When big news happened during the day, CNN had a distinct compet-itive advantage. Moreover, viewers around the country, and eventually around the world, were prepared to pay for timely access to breaking news. Viewership began to increase. As the network news shows faced mounting budget pressures and had to retrench their newsgathering organizations, especially outside of the United States, or become more entertainment-oriented, CNN began filling the void, further cement-ing its dominant position by providing "history in real time." Each viewer translated into more revenue for CNN. Unlike the Superstation, Turner charged cable operators twenty cents per subscriber per month, which added to the growing advertising revenue stream. However, he could now share the expense of his operations across several cable chan-nels, thereby taking advantage of synergies in sales, cable operator rela-tionships, and overhead. And, as he had done with billboards, Turner used unsold advertising time as an opportunity to promote program-ming on his other cable properties.

Short viewer attention spans and a deep understanding that reuse of content could increase profits, a la Walt Disney, led Turner to inau-gurate a new cable channel in late 1981, *CNN Headline News*. Able to provide viewers with an update of international and national events every thirty minutes proved a successful add-on for Turner. It also scared away potential competitors, who began to understand that the determined entrepreneur had carved out a new and profitable busi-ness in what had been their special niche. The two cable news chan-nels together provided sufficient revenue to cover the mostly fixed cost nature of the newsgathering and broadcast business.

Turner did not stop with CNN and CNN Headline News. Grasping the growing power of providing unique content to the nation's cable operators Turner set out to broaden his media empire with the addition of the Metro-Goldwyn-Mayer (MGM) movie library in 1986. Again betting his company, he agreed to pay $1.2 billion for the asset. In time the move would prove masterful but not before putting Turner at the edge of the financial abyss. The MGM library formed the basis for a new cable channel, Turner Network Television—TNT—which was launched in 1988. In 1991, Turner acquired another unique programming library, buying the rights to Hanna-Barbera's many cartoon programs, which became the foundation for the Cartoon Network. Naming Turner its "Man of the Year" in 1991, *Time* magazine praised Turner's leadership of the media revolution over the previous ten years in pioneering the cable television industry and most importantly, bringing the world closer together through CNN.

Turner went on to add other properties before merging his business into the country's largest media conglomerate of the day, Time Warner Corporation, in 1995. It was a crowning achievement for the entrepreneur from Georgia who proved to himself and those around him that entrepreneurial energy combined with a tenacious focus on achieving a far-reaching vision can lead to ground-breaking success. As Turner said, "Making money was always secondary to me. I was interested in the adventure and challenge of it all."[4]

Like many successful entrepreneurs, Ted Turner was neither an angel nor an icon of morality and family values. He was labeled the "Mouth from the South" and "Captain Outrageous" for his frequent outbursts, foul language, constant womanizing, and alcoholism. But, as he matured and grew comfortable that he had achieved the measure of commercial success that seemed to plague him since his father's death, he turned his attention, energy and leadership to more philanthropic goals. With the Cold War still raging, as seen in boycotts by the United States and the Soviet Union of each others' Olympic Games, staged in Los Angeles in 1980 and in Moscow in 1984, Turner originated the first Goodwill Games in 1986 to promote world peace. He lost $26 million on the venture, which hosted over 3,000 athletes from seventy-four countries in Moscow, and then held the games again in 1990 in Seattle, Washington, losing another $44 million. Undeterred, Turner held the games several more times before calling it quits. Then, in a bold attempt to challenge the philanthropic inadequacies of his fellow billionaires Turner earned further accolades by donating $1 billion to various programs of the United Nations in 1997—a further exclamation point on a career spent leading the way.

*   *   *

Were Smith and Turner lucky? Clearly, they were born to advantage and had the good fortune to come of age during a period of rapid technological change. But, their success should not be attributed to luck; far from it. Both men showed huge courage and skill in the face of overwhelming odds and headwinds, and still came in as winners. Big winners. Think about all of the obstacles that stood in their paths as they went up against entrenched competition, regulatory barriers, capital constraints, and armies of naysayers each more emphatic than the next that the task was too hard and would lead to guaranteed failure. Smith and Turner easily could have shredded their family wealth if their business ideas and execution skills had failed. They came close, and both peered into the void at some point, but they always found a way to work through the challenges and come out the other end. Instead, they found ways to persevere always taking the leadership burden upon themselves and moving their organizations forward.

Great ideas don't guarantee success. Smith's hub and spoke overnight delivery system for time sensitive and high value goods, and Turner's "always on" video news service were profound ideas. But while a new breakthrough concept helps position a business for success, it is only the beginning. Someone has to strap the concept onto their back and carry it forward. The most powerful ideas often can withstand more pain, more execution errors, and incoming waves than those offering only marginal improvements, but the ship still needs a captain and the plane still needs a pilot. Effective leadership becomes the most important discriminator between success and failure because someone has to take charge, make the correct strategic decisions, serve as an effective spokesperson for the company and its mission, raise outside capital, recruit and retain other management, attract the initial customers and then continually adjust on the fly as the world evolves and competitive pressures grow.

Getting all of these skills packaged neatly in the same person is extremely unusual. People who excel at strategic vision often lack the patience or soft touch necessary to manage a large organization, especially if it takes on a rapid growth trajectory. Similarly, successful managerial acumen requires a different type of personality than entrepreneurial skill and style. Fred Smith and Ted Turner possessed the entrepreneurial capabilities and leadership skills to develop effective organizations around and beneath them. Their strong personalities and vision attracted talented managers to support the company-building effort. Neither Smith or Turner populated their management teams with "yes men"; instead, they carefully selected people who had entrepreneurial tendencies and superb functional skills that could complement their own deficiencies. These entrepreneurs had the uncanny vision to conceive of something new and fresh, and then had the internal drive and passion to bring their ideas alive, along the way ensuring that enough of the "i's" got dotted and the "t's" got crossed that their foresights seemed easy in hindsight.

CHAPTER 4

NEW HORSES FOR OLD COURSES

Hell, there are no rules here, we are trying to accomplish something.
—Thomas Edison

COMBATING ENTRENCHED COMPETITORS WITH THEIR SUPERIOR balance sheets, experienced management teams, strong brand names, well-oiled supply chains, access to capital, existing cash flow, and long-established customer relationships produces unpleasant roadkill of most new ventures. Attempting to redefine a crowded market by offering a novel service or product remains among the most challenging hurdles in the innovation arena. Only rarely do new concepts emerge with the power to gain enough traction to make a dent in established markets. Sometimes even when the idea is good, the implementation is a struggle and the business fails. Sometimes when the idea is good the competition proves sufficiently nimble to react, copying or modifying and then re-launching its own incarnation of the product or idea that eventually stifles the new entrant. Occasionally, however, an entrepreneur conceives of a new space in the marketplace or finds a way to turn the customer experience on its head in a unique way, giving the new business a foundation for growth and prosperity.

Many people see business innovation as primarily based on new developments in technology or science—a new piece of software, a new computer graphics chip, a new pharmaceutical compound—losing sight of the fact that transformative business innovation mostly comes from new business models applied to existing categories, and not from an expansion of intellectual property. Think of John Mackey's Whole

Foods in grocery-store retailing, Stan Durwood's American Multi-Cinema multiplexes, Michael Dell's built-to-order personal computers, Sam Walton's Wal-Mart stores, Charles Schwab's discount brokerage, or Ken Iverson's Nucor Steel minimills. Although some of these businesses deployed state-of-the-art information technology to support their operations, what distinguished these entrepreneurs was that they developed a new way to tap into a well-established market by identifying a different way of satisfying the customer or meaningfully improving the underlying economics of the business, and thereby carved out their own lucrative niche.

A lot of winning innovation reflects imitation and the transference of successful business approaches from one industry to another. Big-box retailing provides the classic example. Innovative entrepreneurs watched the success in one area, such as Toys "R" Us in the toy store category, and then deployed a similar strategy with office products (Staples) or groceries (Costco). Remember that Henry Ford's automotive assembly line derived from what he had seen being done in the meatpacking industry. And Ted Turner's CNN brought the concept of New York's twenty-four-hour all-news radio stations to television. Open eyes and open minds often provide the first seed of a winning entrepreneurial concept. To get the rest of the way to success requires more; much more.

*   *   *

Most street performers eke out a subsistence living entertaining passersby, perfecting their craft and hoping for small donations of money from well-wishers who appreciate their talent and desire to bring smiles. Part acrobat, part clown, part mime, part juggler, and part magician, a street performer does not give us the "Greatest Show on Earth." To get that blast of childhood entertainment requires a Big Top: three large rings, each featuring its own exciting activity, exotic acts from faraway lands, elephants and tigers, lion tamers, plumed horses, colorful clowns, trapeze artists, death-defying stunts, stately ringmasters with tall black hats and leather boots, human cannonballs arcing over sawdust floors into a large capture net, and streaking spotlights.

The circus has been coming to town for over two hundred years, ever since its founding in Britain in the mid-eighteenth century, and audiences today, mostly families with young children, can still enjoy the traditional mix of circus acts, while eating popcorn and cotton candy, delighting to the sights and sounds of an entertainment spectacle. However, the circus has dwindled as an entertainment form against the onslaught of big-time sporting events, movie megaplexes, Broadway extravaganzas, big-screen TVs, and rock 'n' roll concerts. The MTV generation with its short attention span has seen it all before, with big noise, bright lights, and increasingly outlandish displays. Cutting through the multimedia, high technology clutter takes something truly unique.

Though most circus people are motivated by the love of performing rather than a desire for riches, owning a circus is no longer a pathway to fortune, if it ever was. The high fixed cost of setting up and tearing down the tents, moving a mini-army of performers by truck and train from town to town, feeding and caring for large animals, and meeting the rising promotional costs of trying to attract a youthful audience has, over the years, forced many circus operators to close down. Moreover, in today's politically correct world, animal rights activists further pressure circus operators, who are already running thin on the truly distinctive acts necessary to woo crowds. For at least the past twenty-five years all these trends have suggested that the modern circus business is not a significant money-making proposition.

CRAFTING REINVENTION

Conventional circuses have been in long-term decline due to shrinking audiences, making it very difficult for them to generate profits. Street performers don't make much money either, and never have. Combining the two entertainment forms would seem like a recipe for bankruptcy, but no one bothered to inform Guy Laliberté and Daniel Gauthier. Instead, Laliberté, a former fire-breathing accordionist, and Gauthier, his business-savvy partner, created Cirque du Soleil in 1984, using a $1.7 million arts grant from the Quebec provincial government. Several years earlier the two men had formed a troupe, calling it "Le Club des Talons Hauts" (The High-Heels Club), and had organized the first street performers' festival in Quebec City. The troupe now numbered twenty, including stilt walkers, musicians, clowns, and tumblers. Beneath the bright blue and yellow tent they performed on a stage, not rings, and there were no animals. Their vision was a circus, but of a much different kind.

After a successful tour of Quebec in the summer of 1984, the renamed troupe continued to perform in Canada, but was not profitable.

Operating on a very thin budget, Cirque du Soleil lacked the resources to promote itself or to move away from the traditional constraints of the street performer. Laliberté's group accepted an invitation to the Los Angeles Arts Festival in 1987 and then spent all of its money preparing for the performances; there was not even enough money left for it to get back to Quebec at the end of the run unless it had box-office success. Fortunately, garnering great critical acclaim and lots of free publicity in local newspapers, Cirque du Soleil achieved its goal in Los Angeles. It was enough for the troupe to begin a U.S. tour and to launch its unique business model.

Joined by other street performers and experienced theater directors Cirque du Soleil developed a curious blend of entertainment, combining original music, choreography, colorful costumes, and spellbinding acts from around the world that showcased strength, balance, and movement, sometimes performing high above the crowd, and targeted a more sophisticated, upscale, and older audience than did the traditional three-ring circus. Harmonized around a central theme, Cirque du Soleil was an awe-inspiring production that wowed its spectators. With soaring aerialists, trampolinists, sophisticated clowns, high-wire acts without nets, Cirque du Soleil was as much a Broadway show or an opera as a circus, but demonstrating a higher level of imagination. It had lower operating costs than a traditional circus because it did not use performing animals and had no headline stars. It could also charge a higher ticket price because children and young families no longer made up the primary target market. Cirque du Soleil carved out and then packaged a product for a new entertainment segment, attracting an audience with growing demographics at a higher ticket price point and a lower overall cost structure. It was a winning formula for a successful business. Initially, Laliberté and his team adopted a straightforward business approach focused on creating a unique show and touring it around the world, for up to four years, in their trademark bright-blue and yellow tent. But turning Cirque du Soleil into a business, rather than a series of one-off stage productions, required a totally different mindset and culture. For Laliberté, the challenge was putting in place an organization upfront that would support not just one show, but multiple productions over time, and performances in numerous locations. In addition to the creative aspects of the show—content, lighting, costuming, and music—this would entail hiring people to screen potential acts, training performers, replacing performers who got sick, housing them while they were in training, determining appropriate pay schedules and incentives, leasing practice facilities, and arranging logistics.

Revenue for Cirque du Soleil comes primarily from ticket sales, with the company augmenting this stream by selling corporate sponsorships and concessions. Since Cirque du Soleil targets a sophisticated audience, its ticket prices are consistent with those of high-end Broadway shows, upward of $200 for the top seats. Moreover, the strong brand image of the company, which has become synonymous with the ultimate in creativity, makes an attractive backdrop for large corporations interested in associating with the uniqueness of the performance.

By 1992 Cirque du Soleil had pushed beyond its North American roots and was selling an estimated 500,000 tickets a year for its various touring productions, including shows in Europe and Asia. But, to foster expansion Laliberté decided to seek a permanent venue for one of the shows recognizing that as a resident performance company Cirque du Soleil would have even lower operating costs and the potential for much stronger revenue. The obvious location choice was Las Vegas, where the casino operators understood that a big-name attraction performing two shows a night would bring in thousands of people who would be tempted to stop and play at their slot machines and gaming tables. After discussions with various casino and hotel operators, Laliberté agreed to set up his tent next to the Mirage Hotel and perform one show every night for a year while the hotel constructed a new $20 million, 1,525-seat structure for him. With a permanent presence on the Las Vegas Strip, Cirque du Soleil had not only positioned itself for significant growth and profitability, but had also offloaded to the Mirage the hefty upfront capital expenditures associated with building specially designed venues. This meant that Cirque du Soleil could break-even averaging only 65 percent occupancy. And when the venues sold out, which occurred regularly as word of mouth began pulling in large audiences, the profitability levels became almost as breathtaking as the performances. The ability to amortize the upfront development costs over thousands of performances over many years was reminiscent of one of Disney's approaches to business; he, too, had systematically found ways to spread the early costs of creating his characters and productions, such as by reissuing some of the classic animated feature films every seven years or so. Although Laliberté did not seek to access star performers or indelible characters, the Cirque du Soleil brand guaranteed audiences a similar umbrella denoting a high level of creativity and professionalism and rarely disappointing the audience.

In Las Vegas, Cirque du Soleil had found a huge new audience willing to pay high prices. Soon, Laliberté agreed to long-term performance contracts for other permanent venues in Las Vegas, as well as creating a show for Walt Disney World. The combination of touring shows, permanent Las Vegas establishments, and the company's seemingly unlimited ability to conceive of outstanding new performance content steadily turned Cirque du Soleil from a home for a handful of street performers into an international operation, with many thousands of performers, a significant marketing department, and the challenging logistics of operating around the world every day of the year.

The Cirque du Soleil brand has become golden, as have its profit margins. Annual attendance at its shows throughout the world increased rapidly, numbering over 11 million by 2010 with revenues exceeding $850 million on their way to over $1 billion in 2011 and estimated operating profits of $250 million. Cirque du Soleil has performed in over three hundred cities around the world for over 100 million spectators. To support these immense operations, Cirque du Soleil has grown to a 5,000 person organization, encompassing a wide variety of different vocations, some artistic, some marketing, some logistical.

A simple idea, masterfully implemented, with totally enveloping performances, Cirque du Soleil has become the classic case study of turning an old business model on its head. From its headquarters in Montreal, Cirque du Soleil has reinvented the circus experience, and continually reinvented itself with amazing new productions, always looking to push the envelope so that the organization and its performances never get stale. As its leader, Guy Laliberté, has conceived a distinctive philosophy focused first and foremost on stretching creativity, taking chances, and investing heavily in the quality of the performance. One reason Laliberté, who paid Gauthier an estimated C$400 million for his 50 percent interest in the company in 2000, has kept his company private is to protect its artistic independence, a la Christo. Laliberté felt that most large corporations would never make the upfront production investments or allow him the creative freedom he deemed necessary to keep his company and its increasingly elaborate productions vibrant. With a desire to continually push the limits of "extreme creativity," especially as new competitors emerged who have recognized the potential to tap into his market segment, Laliberté does not let up. Even after Cirque du Soleil's only substantial flop, the $25 million Broadway-like show "Banana Shpeel" in 2010, the organization has jumped back on the bicycle to prove it can overcome failure and launch original productions in 2011 to further the company's New York presence.

More shows, more venues, more profits, more magic from a new type of circus. With approximately twenty-three shows performing around the world from Macau to New York, including seven in permanent Las Vegas venues, the immensity of Cirque du Soleil's entertainment reach continues to grow.

Cirque du Soleil demonstrated a new vision for a long-standing business—the circus. By harvesting the winning factors of the "old way" combined with new concepts the company created substantial distinction in the minds of the customers, leading to a totally new business model that enlarged a market, dictated a higher price point, putting the company on a trajectory of fast growth in what most observers considered a mature industry. With something new to offer and near flawless execution, Cirque du Soleil established a distinct brand image that protects it from potential competitors.

*   *   *

It took the creativity and execution skills of Guy Laliberté to reconceptualize the entertainment experience of the traditional circus and make it a successful enterprise, Finding a new business model to rejuvenate and remake the traditional American coffee shop was hardly a high priority in the restaurant world in the 1980s, but that was because most people could not see beyond the status quo or appreciate the potential bounty. Fortunately for Howard Schultz, no one saw what he saw. Fortunately for all of those Starbuck's addicts around the world, it was Howard Schultz who led the charge.

POURING REINVENTION

Howard Schultz grew up in the housing projects in Brooklyn, New York. His father delivered cloth diapers. An average student in high school, Schultz won a football scholarship attending the less-than-perennial powerhouse Northern Michigan University. After graduating in 1975, Schultz returned to New York, working first as a salesman at Xerox Corporation and then, four years later, joining Swedish industrial company, Perstorp, in their kitchen and housewares operation. Within a few years Schultz had become the division's general manager with twenty people reporting to him.

Schultz's story is reminiscent of the famous account of Ray Kroc, a milkshake machine salesman who had visited the McDonald brothers' hamburger stand in San Bernardino, California in 1954, subsequently buying the business and turning it into one of the largest fast-food restaurant chains in the world. In 1981, Schultz went out to Seattle to visit a small client—Starbucks Coffee, Tea and Spice—that was buying his company's drip coffeemaker. Named after the first mate on the vessel *Pequod* in Herman Melville's classic *Moby Dick* and using a logo derived from a sixteenth-century Norse cutout, Starbucks, located in the trendy Pikes Place Market, sold only whole bean coffee and coffee-related merchandise, but did not serve coffee in the store. The owners, coffee aficionados who had opened their store ten years earlier, focused less on maximizing the value of their business and more on the quality of their coffee beans. They believed that more discerning Americans would migrate from low-end *robusta* coffee to the higher end *arabica* coffee more prevalent in Europe. Schultz quickly understood the market potential of Starbucks' coffee, but it took him about a year to convince the owners that they had identified an attractive market segment and that they could roll out their retail concept across the country. Initially, Schultz's hard-charging, aggressive style did not fit well with the laid-back culture of the founders, who seemed very content with their local operations. Finally, in 1982, Schultz persevered, convincing Starbucks' owners that there was significant growth potential in the high-end coffee market. He left his well-paying job in New York and moved to Seattle to help build-up this five store retail chain. The following year, while on a buying trip in Milan, Schultz was captivated by the city's ubiquitous coffee bars. He recognized that the Italian coffee bar was more than a place to get a cup of coffee; it was the locus of social interaction for the neighborhood. Drinking coffee outside the home was part of daily life in Italy. He returned to the United States convinced that there was an enormous opportunity to bring the Italian coffee bar concept to America. Based on the estimated 20,000 espresso bars in Italy, Schultz saw enormous potential in the United States for Starbucks to leverage its existing reputation for fine

coffee into a chain of Italian-styled coffee bars unlike the more traditional "diners" or coffee shops that most Americans frequented. The
unappetizing picture of linoleum floors, Formica tables, scratchy Juke
boxes, white mugs, shoddy cardboard containers, greasy spoons, old
waitresses, white-bread menus, and three-day-old cakes lent itself to a
different era, far removed from the increasing affluence of the upwardly
mobile professional class that Schultz sought to cater to. Schultz understood that in America, as in Italy, there was a need for an oasis from
the outside world where people could meet and take a break from their
normal routines while enjoying an affordable luxury—a cup of really
good coffee.

Although Schultz was an excellent salesman, he could not convince
the Starbucks' owners to launch this new venture as they preferred to
stay in the business of grinding coffee beans, not serving coffee. But
Schultz believed he had a winning idea. By the time Starbucks opened
its sixth store in 1984, he had gotten permission to carve out a small
space for brewing and serving espresso. Schultz had established a toe-
hold, and his persistence was about to pay off.

However, like many entrepreneurs, Schultz was anxious to roll
out his idea. Unable to tolerate the slow-paced decision making of
Starbuck's owners, he quit his job and started his own chain of coffee houses, named *Il Giornale,* after the Italian newspaper. Schultz
raised $400,000 in start-up capital in 1985, including $150,000
from the owners of Starbucks, and then an incremental $1.65 mil-
lion to launch eight espresso bars. However, investors showed little
interest in financing the growth of a new coffee shop business, and
fund-raising proved to be a huge challenge for Schultz due in part
because coffee sales in the United States were stagnant at the time
with the rapid growth in the markets for soft drinks and bottled
water, coupled with the generic dislike many venture capitalists had
for the restaurant business, especially a project with little obvious
competitive advantage. Schultz demonstrated tremendous commitment and perseverance, visiting over two hundred investors before
securing sufficient risk capital to get his new business concept off
the ground.

Although Schultz's initial implementation —featuring opera music,
paninis, baristas wearing bow ties, and menus written in Italian—
proved "too Italian," he quickly moderated the theme making changes
to fit the local market. Within six months of the first store's opening,

Il Giornale opened a second location in Seattle, and then a third store in Vancouver, British Columbia. Business was booming, proving Schultz's thesis that Americans would enjoy cappuccinos and café lattes, especially when served by knowledgeable and friendly baristas. In early 1987, the founders of Starbucks decided to sell out, and Schultz raised $3.8 million to buy their business, combining it with *Il Giornale* and phasing out the Italian name.

However, Starbucks, under Schultz, was not an overnight success. The company struggled to meet vendor payment schedules and payroll. Schultz did not take a salary for the first year, and the business lost over $2 million during its first three years as they migrated the Starbucks stores to restaurants and began to roll out new stores. There were many times when Schultz felt that his company might not make it. At one point, his father-in-law flew out to Seattle to try to persuade him to "give up this hobby and get a job," but Schultz understood that the difference between winning and losing, between success and failure, was perseverance. He was relentless, driven by his desire to win and by his memories of growing up in a Brooklyn housing project. He was driven to succeed.

Howard Schultz became passionate about coffee and the coffee-drinking experience, stating, "You can't fake this. Any business leader in any organization knows that you can't build greatness if you aren't obsessed with what you are doing."[1] He was consumed by the notion that his idea would work. To support rapid growth he raised more money, recognizing that there were few barriers to entry in his business other than superior store location and a quality brand name. He wanted to position Starbucks as the preeminent high-end coffee company while consistently delivering a satisfying customer experience that encouraged repeat business and supported premium prices.

To ensure high quality Schultz and his team established an organization and infrastructure to enable their growth, from the sourcing of coffee beans, developing the product packaging, recruiting and training the baristas, creating the store environment, managing the perishable inventory, pricing, selecting ideal store locations, and creating the public relations story to establish Starbucks as a brand. Surprisingly, Starbucks spent very little on advertising in its early years, especially compared with other consumer goods companies.

To support planned growth while providing a differentiated customer experience, Schultz recognized that Starbucks would succeed only if the company met the expectations of its employees, and through them, the expectations of the customer, pointing out that "Starbucks is not in the coffee business, but in the people business."[2] Unlike most companies in the restaurant business that pay their workers minimum wage with poor health care benefits, if any, Starbucks became dedicated to satisfying its employees. Understanding that happy employees would make for happy customers, Schultz implemented two novel concepts for a business staffed primarily by part-time employees: comprehensive health care benefits and stock options for everyone. Soon, Starbucks spent more on employee health insurance than on coffee beans. Staffed by dedicated workers, Starbucks reduced turnover and lowered training costs, much as Henry Ford had done in 1914 when he shocked the world by nearly doubling his autoworkers' pay to $5.00 per day. The company's employee stock-option plan, Bean Stock, was available to all employees with over six months of tenure who worked more than twenty hours a week, and its initial option grants at $6 a share grew to a value of $132 a share within five years; an employee earning $20,000 a year part-time had an equity position in the company worth $50,000. Real money bred real dedication as well as a high level of employee job satisfaction that customers could feel when they entered the store.

Despite his desire for rapid growth and his lack of interest in the dilution from selling shares in his company, franchising was not for Schultz. He wanted the company to own all the Starbucks stores, believing that this would make it easier to maintain quality over the entire customer experience and nurture a common corporate culture. But, doing this meant that he needed even more outside money to identify new locations, outfit these stores, and build the local traffic. In 1988, Starbucks raised $3.9 million from wealthy individuals, and in 1990 the company tapped into the venture capital community receiving $13.5 million of new equity. When the company had its IPO in June 1992, Starbucks operated only one hundred stores and had a mere $57 million of revenue.

In addition to fund-raising, Schultz needed to attract an experienced leadership team to manage the growth of the business. Intelligently, he recruited highly skilled executives for key positions, including a CFO and COO, and added managers from fast-food restaurant chains and consumer packaged goods companies. Schultz said:

Many business visionaries have failed as leaders because they could not execute. Processes and systems, discipline and efficiency are needed to create a foundation before creative ideas can be implemented and entrepreneurial vision can be realized.[3]

Within five years of its founding Starbucks became a phenomenon, growing at an incredible rate on its pathway to over 17,000 stores and operations in fifty countries. Howard Schultz and his team had reinvented the coffee shop. Commenting on his success Schultz said: "If I took you to where I grew up, the odds of me going from there to here are unfathomable. But, it happened."[4]

Under Schultz's leadership Starbucks became a destination, an inviting place to hang out between work and home, a place to listen to calming music while smelling the coffee aroma and getting your daily caffeine fix and to catch up on your email while waiting for a friend or colleague. Today, Starbucks is hugely successful, with annual revenues exceeding $10 billion and operating profits totaling over $1 billion, even after disappointing financial results in 2008. Founder Howard Schultz, who had stepped back from overseeing day-to-day operations in 2000, reengaged as CEO, believing that his company had diluted its core offerings, having lost the plot, stretching too hard for growth, and losing its focus. Mostly, Schultz recognized that the ability to collect premium prices from the Starbucks experience was in danger of wilting unless the company could recapture its distinctiveness, especially as competitors, such as Dunkin Donuts and McDonald's, began to make inroads. He pushed the company and its 120,000 worldwide employees to re-institutionalize the high touch customer service and superior-quality approach that had propelled its early growth and phenomenal success. However, in the process of revitalizing Starbucks Schultz was forced to lay off approximately 550 employees, reversing one of his core business principles and to shutter about six hundred stores. Even Starbucks' meteoric growth was not flawless, and it took the courage and leadership of its founder to make the hard decisions necessary to help the company retrench, regain its form, and then march ahead.

*   *   *

Great French scientist Louis Pasteur claimed that his success was tied solely to his tenacity. Thomas Edison's famous adage suggests that genius is mostly perspiration, not inspiration. Laliberté and Schultz needed both insight and perseverance to take their new companies from concept to success. Both attributes proved defining. As entrepreneurs they brought new business models to previously mature markets, riding the wave of American, and now international, increasing standards of living. By providing customers a high quality experience, they could charge premium prices. These two entrepreneurs sweated every detail, exerting diligent control over the customer experience and the organization tasked with its delivery, creating competitive advantage, not through a superior new technology but through solid execution of a well-honed strategy.

CHAPTER 5

NEXT-MOVER ADVANTAGE

You've got to know the rules to break them.
—Alexander McQueen

POPULAR BUSINESS LITERATURE TEACHES THE VIRTUES OF NEW
enterprises running to the front of the pack in an attempt to grab
market share before customers become wedded to one vendor versus
another. This strategy often makes sense because the early participants
build entry barriers for competitors and exit barriers for customers.
But there are numerous examples of fast-followers and companies that
offered superior products, services, or execution capability and out-
ran the pioneers, leaving them with proverbial arrows in their backs.
Sometimes new technology emerges that can help to create competitive advantage and tailor new innovations. Sometimes watching and
learning, and then correcting or adjusting with a different strategy sets
up a different path. Remember that Facebook followed MySpace, Bill
Gate's Microsoft followed Gary Kildall's Digital Research, and Phil
Knight's Nike followed Adidas (not to mention Converse). First movers may have an advantage, but this doesn't guarantee them the pole
position forever or relieve them of the need to constantly look over their
shoulder to see who is gaining on them. Even if you run to the front,
it is hard to stay there. New ideas on top of great execution behind
innovative leadership, especially if you couple them with a devotion to
employees that creates the power of a coordinated team, can surpass
the entrenched front runners. By running marathons versus sprints,
innovators come out ahead. By building an organization with depth,

cult-like devotion, and attention to those who create the distinctive customer experience entrepreneurs stay ahead.

*   *   *

The superb entrepreneur Sir Richard Branson once joked that "if you want to be a millionaire, start with a billion dollars and launch a new airline." Historically, there may be worse businesses than passenger airlines, but not many. Aviation is an industry which over its entire lifetime has been a net destroyer of capital, where most of the customers despise the service provider, where government regulations and labor unions constrain the operators' ability to maneuver, where ongoing threats of international terrorism that started with hijackings in the 1970s make protection of the aircraft and its passengers a major concern, and where the volatility of jet fuel prices makes cost control extremely challenging. It is hard to imagine why anyone would want to start, much less manage, an airline, but some people find it rather sexy to have an airline, and they are able to get into the business without huge amounts of capital, despite the industry's history of losing money most of the time. Fortunately they do, or we would all spend much more time riding on trains, buses, and in automobiles.

In the early days of carrying people (versus mail), circa the 1940s, airline passengers dressed in their most fashionable clothes when flying. They were served meals on fine china, with linen tablecloths, and real silverware, not plastic; they sat in comfortable seats, and had plenty of legroom. Flying was a great adventure reminiscent of the days of luxurious cruise liners and first-class train travel. Early pioneers such as Juan Trippe's Pan-American Airways and Howard Hughes' Trans World Airlines shrunk the world. The advent of the jet engine on commercial aircraft in the 1950s, computerized reservation systems in the 1960s, and fixed ticket prices approved by the federal government permitted passenger airlines to make reasonable returns on their capital. However, all that changed beginning in the 1970s, first with the energy crisis that began in 1973, followed by deregulation of U.S. airlines in 1978. Once airlines had the flexibility to determine their own routes and ticket prices, they slowly turned a one-time nicely profitable business into a commodity-like service with high, (mostly) fixed cost structures as low entry barriers brought considerable competition and increased capacity into the industry. While deregulation was beneficial in lowering fares and expanding service around the country, it also forced a complete restructuring of the passenger airline industry. Industry profits went down, and many airlines found merger partners to bolster their route structures and streamline their overhead. Some airlines proved incapable of adjusting to the new economic reality and disappeared into bankruptcy as their accumulated debt and inability to generate profits made them uncompetitive. In an effort to improve their economics many airlines implemented hub-and-spoke systems, like those developed by Federal Express, as a new model for moving people. The concept was simple and helped drive efficiency, but it also meant that travelers often experienced extended delays and missed connections, as many itineraries funneled passengers into large hubs, such as Chicago's O'Hare and Atlanta's Hartsfield airports, where they then connected to other flights taking them to their final destination.

EXPANDING MARKETS

But for some entrepreneurs, low price provided the cornerstone for delivering attractive customer value. This was the case for Herb Kelleher, a practicing lawyer in Texas in 1967. His client at the time, Roland King, who operated an air taxi service, recognized an untapped market opportunity in transporting people the one hundred and ninety to two hundred and fifty miles between Houston, Dallas–Fort Worth, and San Antonio, Texas. The distance between these cities was not so great, and budget-conscious travelers and businesspeople sometimes decided to make the drive or take the bus rather than fly on one of the prevailing carriers—Braniff International Airways and Texas International Airlines—which were known for high ticket prices and mediocre service. King and Kelleher saw the chance to introduce low-cost passenger air service between these rapidly growing cities, and they developed a distinct business model to ensure success. Since the proposed routes never crossed state boundaries, King and Kelleher applied for and were awarded a Texas license for their new company, Southwest Airlines, to provide intrastate air service between the three cities, bypassing the requirement of a federal license and its hefty regulatory burden. The entrenched carriers on these routes accessed their big balance sheets and had an army of lawyers sue Southwest Airlines, using every imaginable legal and political weapon hoping to destroy the start-up enterprise before it could launch service. After a costly and protracted legal battle that was eventually settled by the U.S. Supreme Court, Southwest Airlines prevailed and finally was allowed to start service in 1970.

King and Kelleher were joined by Lamar Muse, an experienced airline executive who became Southwest Airlines' president, as they went to work creating their new airline. During the first half of 1971, Southwest Airlines raised $7 million of equity and $17 million in debt—an extraordinary amount of money especially in that period—recognizing that they had tremendous upfront costs and would likely experience a long period of operating losses as they built their passenger base. This fund-raising success was a testament to the flair of the founders and the potential of their proposed business model.

In the midst of a poor economy and an industry recession, Southwest Airlines succeeded in purchasing three new Boeing 737 aircraft at advantageous prices, taking advantage of generous vendor financing, proving once again that sometimes the best time to start a new business is when economic conditions are poor. The Boeing 737 required fewer crew members than aircraft used by Southwest Airlines' competitors and its more modern design necessitated less maintenance. Their initial routes used Dallas' older Love Field and Houston's Hobby Airport, avoiding the new larger airports used by the competition, that were located many miles from the city center. The smaller downtown airports were closer to passengers' likely ultimate destination and landing/takeoff and gate fees were much lower than at the newer airports. Southwest Airlines could begin to construct the low-cost operating structure that would be critical to its long-term success. Most important was the company's recognition that its mission was to provide considerably improved service at a fraction of the cost of the competition. Southwest Airlines decided to price their service at a level that would fill its planes while still covering their operating costs. At the initial fares of $20, Southwest immediately broadened the market by creating a much faster alternative to bus service. With the help of experienced advertising executives Southwest distanced themselves from the stodgy image of Braniff and Texas International by creating an irreverent publicity campaign that suggested a different kind of flying experience for passengers. As with Federal Express, catchy advertising slogans created a distinct brand image and set the company apart from its stuffy competitors.[1] Having looked at the poor practices of the passenger airlines serving these routes and seen what not to do, Southwest Airlines offered its passengers frequent service between its favored airports at low fares, on new airplanes, with fast ticketing processes, featuring attractive flight attendants wearing hot pants, and serving inexpensive drinks. It proved a powerful recipe for building clientele.

Further supporting the implementation of Southwest's strategy was an unusual personnel selection process designed to attract a personality type who could deliver the high level of personalized customer service the airline wanted to provide. Southwest understood that service levels could be high even with low fares and limited frills if their employees showed a commitment to the success of the airline, such as undertaking multiple jobs. Southwest looked for job applicants with a sense of humor, an ability and desire to take initiative, and outgoing personalities. The underlying philosophy was to focus on attracting employees with the right attitude and then train them in the necessary skill set. Like Howard Schultz's Starbucks, Southwest Airlines grasped that happy employees are more likely to stay with the company, reducing the need for recruiting and cutting the cost of training replacements. Moreover, dedicated employees enhance corporate productivity while extending a helping hand to customers.

Slowly, Southwest Airlines began to increase its customer load levels as it struggled to reach breakeven in its first year of operation. The competition fought back hard, replicating Southwest's route structures, lowering fares, and increasing their advertising programs. Southwest responded in kind with further price reductions, service expansions, more creative advertising, and publicity stunts to attract attention.[2] These combined actions expanded the market even more, attracting additional air travelers and improving Southwest's aircraft capacity utilization.

By 1973, Southwest Airlines had reached profitability, carrying over 500,000 passengers that year and steadily ramping-up service frequencies, while further developing a business model that would become the template for low-cost passenger carriers all over the world. With a limited, relatively short-haul route structure with average flying times of forty to fifty minutes, Southwest could standardize on the modern Boeing 737 aircraft making maintenance easier, lowering its spare-part inventory, reducing maintenance training costs, substituting its flight crews and pilots, and facilitating faster turnaround time from arrival to the next departure. Its point-to-point routing system versus the hub-and-spoke architecture of its competitors further minimized waiting times at airports. Instead of boarding its passengers by row, Southwest instituted a first-come, first-served approach that accelerated the boarding process, and it never had to deal with first class passengers since it only had one level of service. By minimizing the time its planes sat on the ground, Southwest could make the best use of its significant investment in its most expensive asset, the aircraft. Instead of serving meals on flights, the company offered only snacks, mostly peanuts, and beverages, meaning that it took less time to cater and clean aircraft between flights. Since Southwest did not offer assigned seating it relied on reusable boarding cards. Over time, Southwest's aircraft were flying twice the number of flights per day as the competition. To enhance employee loyalty and align its interests with those of its workforce, Southwest Airlines successfully implemented profit-sharing and employee stock-ownership plans.

Lamar Muse retired from Southwest Airlines in 1979, turning the leadership responsibility over to general counsel Herb Kelleher. Kelleher had a distinct personality combining a ruthless competitive streak with strong people motivation skills. He created a powerful corporate culture that nurtured its workforce, believing that loyal employees would translate into happy customers. Within the company Kelleher became iconic, less so for his co-founder status, and mostly for his warmth, good nature, charismatic, outgoing attitude, warrior spirit, and the obvious affection and gratitude he felt for all of the company's employees. Kelleher would show up on a Southwest Airline flight, not as a passenger, but to help out with the luggage or assist the flight attendants. He would appear at airport hangars and worksites glad-handing employees and thanking them for doing what they did every day. Sometimes Kelleher showed his unconventional side, dressing up in costumes or participating in publicity stunts, all of which furthered the airlines image while creating a work environment that was fun for employees and passengers. He was that rare leader who understood that corporate culture is an integral part of a winning business strategy, that employees who come to work engaged and thrilled with the company and its leadership will be more productive and become the best sales people for the company with its customers. As Kelleher said, "Employees come first, customers come second."

What started as a glimmer in the entrepreneurial eyes of its founders as an idea to launch a new airline, going up against entrenched, substantially larger competition, turned into one of the great business success stories, copied around the world in other countries and regions where a low-price value proposition supported by a comprehensive low-cost operating structure can generate consistent profitability. However, low cost through no-frills approach alone is not sufficient for long-term success in the passenger airline business. It was Southwest Airlines' integrated system for maximizing flights, expanding frequencies from its airports, amortizing the costs of aircraft, pilots, and crew with an employee base purposely selected and trained to make flying fun that coalesced into a winning formula in an industry that most people thought ruinous. Many other airlines have tried to compete in the United States against Southwest Airlines but nearly all have failed to bring together the totality of elements that make Southwest Airlines unique. Moreover, the strong leadership of the entrepreneurial founders and Herb Kelleher's thirty-seven year tenure at the top provided continuity and cultural strength and further cemented the company's distinctiveness. Today, Southwest Airlines flies over 100 million passengers a year to over sixty different cities in America, is regularly recognized for its high service levels, and is acknowledged annually as one of the best companies to work for in the United States. Not bad for a little airline from Texas.

*   *   *

Although Larry Page and Sergey Brin never completed their Ph.D.'s in computer science, they did manage to develop and implement one of the most powerful business models ever. As graduate students at Stanford in the late 1990s, they reluctantly formed Google, a new venture meant to take advantage of their concept for a superior Internet search engine that they believed would provide faster access to more relevant content than the many prevailing service offerings. They were right. Although great technology often becomes a strong barrier to others and a competitive differentiator, it proved to be an insufficient condition for business success in the fast-growing, albeit hotly contested, Internet search engine space. Moreover, the glorified theory of "first-mover advantage" which holds that a market sector's total profitability gravitates toward the company that establishes itself first, clearly has not played out among Internet search engines.

ADVERTISING: THE KILLER APP

Page and Brin recognized that as the number of web pages began expanding rapidly, it was becoming increasing difficult for people to efficiently search the World Wide Web. The popular search engines of the day, including Yahoo!, AltaVista, Excite, HotBot, and others, responded to inquiries with search indices that were based on keyword frequency. It was easy for website developers to game the system by loading their web pages with numerous mentions of key words. Page and Brin had a better idea. Using advanced mathematical techniques they crafted a unique set of algorithms that would deliver search results tied to the quantity and deemed relevancy of links from other web pages, recognizing that this approach would lead to higher quality, more applicable responses. At a time when the Internet bubble was inflating on Wall Street and any Internet-related venture captured easy financing, Google was able to raise millions of dollars from several of Silicon Valley's leading venture capital firms and angel investors based on a limited business plan and leadership from two smart guys who had no business experience.

Page and Brin's search engine proved very effective and quickly developed a following. The original Google business model was incredibly simple, but not especially lucrative. Although Google had its own website, revenue generation came from license fees, as Google sought to power the Internet searching function of established portal companies, such as Yahoo! At the time, Google was primarily a technology wholesaler to other companies that interfaced directly with users. While licensing models sometimes provide nice revenue streams and attractive returns on capital invested, they are rarely the foundation for long-term economic bonanzas. Fortunately for Google, their technology proved to be so superior to that being used by the other search engines, and their minimalist home page loaded so quickly, that they rapidly developed a leadership position in Internet search.

However, the great innovation commercialized by Google was not originated by Google. Instead, it came from a company started in 1998 called Overture, Inc. which understood that advertising represented the most attractive way to monetize the increasing number of eyeballs focused on web pages. Overture's insight was to sell web-page advertising space that was tied to the content of the search. As opposed to "banner ads," which end-users considered a nuisance, targeted advertising, based directly on the topics they were interested in was worth a lot. Overture sold ad placement to the highest bidder of individual keywords and phrases so that their services would show up toward the top of the list of any relevant search topic, and then the advertiser would pay if the user clicked on the link or advertisement. Paid search became the best way for search engine providers to generate revenue in Internet-land, where end users expect to get everything for free.

Google launched its own improved version of Overture, called AdWords, in 2000. Leveraging its superior search engine, Google had become the preferred choice for users who wanted the most efficient and effective search results. Coupled with the success of the "click through" advertising model, Google had a real business. As the company improved the quality of the search experience, it continued to take market share, making it also the most effective place for advertisers to concentrate their online spend. Although Google's market share differs across the globe, today, it performs roughly two-thirds of all Internet searches, China excluded. In a relatively short time span, the word "google" entered the language, becoming a verb form synonymous with "search" and such a strong brand name—much like Kleenex, FedEx, Xerox, Band-Aid, and Hoover in the past—that it became generic for its function.

In addition to providing advertising to users in search of information, Google added a new service in 2003, AdSense, that provided advertising on websites of original content. If someone went to a hip-hop music website, Google provided advertising on that web page tailored to those interested in that topic. Called "contextual paid listings," Google furthered its advertising-driven services, targeting advertising to the most interested users.

While Google revolutionized the online advertising business by re-architecting the relationship between advertisers and Internet users, it did not base its success solely on its Internet search algorithms. With a self-defined mission to organize the world's information and make it universally accessible and useful, Google's founders understood that as the Internet proliferated and became a global information utility, the company would have to create a truly international business powered by the most sophisticated computer infrastructure. That would cost serious money. Fortunately, the paid-search business model proved to be tremendously profitable.

At inception, Google's founders understood this prospective need and began to create a proprietary, scalable, information network engineered to move large quantities of data as fast as possible. Their strategy was not only to provide great search results, but to provide them extremely fast. When you search for information on Google's website, it tells you how many sites it found and how many milliseconds it took the system to respond. Both features are important to the company's mission. Google guards the details of its current multibillion dollar IT infrastructure, but its numerous server farms around the world contain an estimated one million made-to-order units networked together with specially developed data-management and operating-system software, plus artificial intelligence that is customized to enhance the retrieval and management of massive amounts of information. Today, Google's IT system has to support several billion searches a day in over forty languages. Google seeks and has attained competitive advantage and improved profitability by finding ways to increase processing speed, lower electricity usage, and reduce headcount. Although Google sometimes can get the computer performance it needs by buying servers and software "off-the-shelf," it is not averse to "rolling its own" by designing proprietary software and database management systems, creating artificial intelligence algorithms, and buying made-to-order hardware if the performance gains justify the expense.

Part of Google's uniqueness stems from the guiding principles of its founders, whose unconventional approach to business further defines the company's strategy and effectiveness. Even in the often nonconformist world of Silicon Valley, Google stands out for a number of eccentricities that define and reinforce its corporate culture. To start, Google's founders were joined in 2001 by a seasoned corporate executive, Eric Schmidt, who had a high level of technology competence and a successful business track record, to provide guidance and gravitas. While Schmidt was hired as the Chairman and CEO, he, Brin and Page formed a leadership triumvirate of varying skills and loosely-defined organizational responsibilities. Recently, Page took back the CEO mantle, but how that will change the senior managerial dynamics remains unclear.

A more detailed definition of the Google culture can be found in its "Statement of Principles," which include such tenets as "you can make money without doing evil," "you can be serious without a suit," "focus on the user and all else will follow," and "great just isn't good enough." The company clearly strives for an unusually high level of excellence. Google's distinctive hiring methodologies filter for only the best and brightest, its extensive corporate campus—the Googleplex—promotes high levels of productivity and group behavior, and its culture has been engineered from inception to encourage innovation.

In its active efforts to foster creativity, Google resembles the highly diversified industrial conglomerate 3M, which often stands out as the leading example of the large multinational company that has long understood the need to promote innovation. With programs aimed to ensure that its product lines remain fresh and that its product development people have time to be creative (by allowing them to dedicate a portion of their time to self-defined projects), 3M has grown and broadened itself for over one hundred years. Google has a similar philosophy. It sees an opportunity to change the world of information, and to achieve this objective it has a clear policy pushing its people to take risks, develop new ideas and products, and nurture a collaborative environment that encourages inventiveness. Google's engineers can spend up to 20 percent of their time pursuing their own projects. This freedom has led to numerous new product initiatives that further the company's broader mission. Google doesn't penalize its people if their ideas fail, recognizing that failure, especially if it comes quickly, is part of a risk-taking philosophy that helps prevent the organization from becoming stale and overly cautious.

Google bases its business model on driving more web traffic to create more gross advertising revenue. Much as Intel invests directly in businesses that create demand for more microprocessors, Google aims to tie users more closely to its software and services, both online and wirelessly. The consistently growing multibillion dollar profit engine from its advertising business has allowed the company to subsidize many new products and to make acquisitions, including Gmail, Google Maps, Google Docs, the Android operating system for mobile devices, YouTube, and Google Books. Each product offering increases the amount of information that Google can search, use for incremental advertising placement, and ensure that its customers don't spend time or money with other software and information service providers. The approach is brilliant from an offensive position and mandatory from a defensive position given that its turf is under increasing attack from Microsoft, Apple, Amazon.com, and others.

Silicon Valley is a competitive and expensive place to build a new business. Most new start-ups fail, sometimes generating a great deal of publicity. Employee turnover runs much higher than most places in America, because job-hopping to the newest "hot company" is the norm. In this environment, creating an employee-focused culture, especially for a business with the growth trajectory of Google, makes obvious sense. It requires more than a large paycheck and a hefty stock-option package to retain quality talent, and Google succeeds here, too.

The corporate culture was designed from the outset to keep the company on the forefront of technology by attracting and retaining the smartest people with an interest in managing the world's information. A rigorous and unconventional recruiting routine, Google's fancy cafeteria and other perks, and a general philosophy that fosters innovation empower its workforce.

The Google business model succeeds because the company combined great search technology, an excellent delivery infrastructure, and a talented workforce anxious to demonstrate creativity and innovativeness. These pieces join up tightly, and are extremely challenging for other companies to duplicate. Copying only one or two of the strategic strands won't create a viable competitor. The company's huge financial success and consistently strong growth provides an ever-increasing cash cushion that supports the company's objective to change the world. As Eric Schmidt has said, "Making money is a technology to pay for it."

* * *

Attorney Herb Kelleher never expected that he would build the country's most profitable airline. Graduate students Sergey Brin and Larry Page had a better idea for a search engine, but that business model morphed into something far more exciting. Entrepreneurs get epiphanies, but rarely are they blueprints for building successful businesses, much less those that totally alter buying patterns and achieve luminary status. Their business plans did not grow out of whole cloth but instead took time to develop, undergoing considerable alteration along the way. What distinguished these entrepreneurs and their companies was how they adjusted their strategies to take advantage of market and structural changes in the world around them, incorporating other people's good ideas, and then creating multiple competitive advantages so that their businesses continued to successfully evolve. Most impressively, each assembled a company that, over time, wove together several strategic strands to form a far more profitable and defensible business. All of these entrepreneurs entered highly competitive markets necessitating that they each develop a clever pathway whether in the form of low cost structures with high service levels, or paid search.

Moreover, the founders of these companies recognized that their workforces, if treated well, would provide a distinguishing incremental asset beyond their planes and search engines, furthering their positions versus competitors and also supporting the economics of their businesses. From the outset each company placed an unusual emphasis on supporting its personnel, encouraging their independence and creativity, and delegating authority. Landing a job at Southwest Airlines or Google means that the applicant had demonstrated a high level of cultural fit with his or her new employer, which further binds the people and the company. Establishing a supportive, fun, focused, people-oriented culture is not the hardest thing, yet most companies remain too shortsighted to spend the time getting this right.

CHAPTER 6

FAILURE IS AN OPTION

Failure is simply an opportunity to begin again, this time more intelligently.

—Henry Ford

MILTON HERSHEY'S FIRST TWO CANDY COMPANIES WENT BANKRUPT before he found a recipe for a distinctive confection, caramels. It was only later that he went into the chocolate business and became a household name. Walt Disney's first cartoon factory and second entrepreneurial venture, Laugh-O-Gram Films, folded not long after it started. His third start-up company continues to flourish. Henry Ford's first two car companies flopped, though the second one was restarted by others and became Cadillac. His third attempt profoundly influenced society. We only care about these failures because in each case the entrepreneur regrouped, having learned from prior mistakes, persevered, and launched a new venture that had considerable success.

Building a business from a raw start is hard, risky work. Nevertheless, entrepreneurs keep coming. The excitement of the chase, the opportunity to win fame and fortune, the potential to change the world creates a continuous stream of corporate creators.

Although the process of innovation is not always pretty and rarely successful, a staggering number of people believe that they have the next great idea for a business, a new creative way of doing something, or a passion to make their mark. Sadly, most are unable to meet their goals, failing for a nearly infinite number of reasons, including not actually having a very good idea, running into tough headwinds economically or from a regulatory perspective, an inability to raise sufficient financing to implement their plans, short-term greed, organizational dysfunction, inadequate market demand, product development snafus, competitive pressures, or maybe all of the above.

The failures remind us how challenging it is for a new venture to break through, gain traction, and build scale while creating a foundation for sustainability. When screening potential new investments most venture capitalists focus on the quality and experience of the management team, the proprietary nature of the product or service, the potential size of the market, the capital needs to grow the business to positive cash flow, and that the profit potential inherent in the business model will reap the expected return on investment. These factors come packaged neatly together only a small percentage of the time. Far more often only one or two of the desired criteria exist, lessening the probability of an attractive result. Failure remains the most likely outcome. Some businesses fail because their strategies are not sufficiently differentiated or their management made some poor decisions or the operational implementation proved shoddy or the capital markets took a break at the wrong time. Inevitably, lots of things go wrong when trying to build a business from the ground up. The potholes faced by most organizations become debilitating because the primary resources, both financial and managerial, cannot adjust in real-time to negative news, bad events, or poor execution.

Synchronizing all of the facets of a young business presents its own challenges. Successful entrepreneurs have to harmonize attractive product features, sufficient manufacturing capacity, efficient distribution channels, a capable and incentivized management team and employee base, leading-edge information technology systems, and a reasonable internal cost structure to bring to market a differentiated product or service at an acceptable price point, and accomplish all of this with limited financial resources. Their task is hard, and their journey is exciting.

Every year and every business cycle new ventures form across numerous industries and around the world. Only a small percent find their footing. The media loves to accentuate these failures, seemingly taking pride in admonishing those who fall short trumpeting their financial losses without understanding that capitalism comes with risk as well as opportunity. High-profile start-ups that failed after consuming hundreds of millions of dollars gained special notoriety in the "dot.bomb era," led by Webvan (an online grocery retailer that consumed $800 million of private and public investor money), and Pets.com (one of four large online pet supply companies which chewed through $300 million). Hundreds of other start-ups launched at the same time with great ambition and enthusiasm also could not generate profits or distinguish themselves sufficiently to justify their existence. They have all gone away, expensive experiments and valiant efforts that did not work, but they left behind many dozens that carved out a niche and grew into successful enterprises, including such notable companies as Amazon.com, eBay, Netflix, and Priceline.com. The nature of capitalism and basic economic principles mandate that it has to be this way; some new ventures will work while others will not. Mostly though, the failures remind us to applaud the successes.

* * *

Dean Kamen stands today as one of America's foremost inventors. Despite never graduating college, he has had enormous success devising new products that people wanted and has turned that business model into a successful enterprise. For nearly his entire life Kamen has functioned outside of the mainstream, comfortable that his eccentricities have not stilted his creative acumen or spirit. Born on Long Island in 1951, Kamen was a classic baby-boomer though an unusual child. Not very interested in school, but passionate about science and engineering, he spent a large chunk of his time developing lighting systems for New York City museums and other institutions, earning substantial income for a teenager. He turned his parents' basement into his laboratory and machine shop. When the space became too small, he sent his parents on a cruise, hired an architect and a bulldozer, and excavated the backyard to increase his workspace.

INVENTION IS NOT INNOVATION

Kamen proved very successful at developing ideas for new products. His early success was with medical equipment. He came up with a device that delivered a precise dose of medicine to a patient, and then the first drug infusion test, followed by a precise-flow portable insulin pump to help diabetics. At age 31, Kamen sold his medical pump business to Baxter Healthcare for $30 million and used the money to create a new company in Manchester, New Hampshire, called DEKA Research and Development Corporation. DEKA's primary objective was to work with clients to develop new products and to earn a royalty stream from the technology it invented. DEKA did not get involved in manufacturing or marketing, leaving that dimension of the business to the corporations who had licensed DEKA's intellectual property. Kamen achieved another breakthrough in 1987 when DEKA designed a quiet, inexpensive, portable kidney dialysis machine. A multimillionaire by the time he was forty-nine, Kamen had been granted over one hundred and fifty patents and had earned the National Medal of Technology, the United States' highest honor for inventors. In 2005, Kamen was inducted into the prestigious National Inventors Hall of Fame.

With the profits from his business Kamen enjoyed life his way. He designed his own home in an unusual shape, and built secret passages. He owned expensive cars, large antique machinery, a wind turbine, planes, and helicopters. He even bought an island off the Connecticut coast and then proceeded to create its own currency, giving one bill the value of pi. On most days he wore the same outfit: blue jeans, matching denim shirt, and work boots.

But Kamen was also philanthropic, and in 1989 he organized and funded his own nonprofit organization in New Hampshire, which he called FIRST (For Inspiration and Recognition of Science and Technology), whose goal was to get children interested in science and engineering. Cleverly, Kamen used FIRST to establish and manage annual robotics competitions around the country pairing volunteers, local company sponsors, and high school students. Today, over 250,000 students take part in FIRST competitions, assisted by approximately 90,000 volunteers.

In the late 1980s, Kamen had watched a man in a wheelchair try to get over a street curb. It was impossible. Over the next eight years at a cost of approximately $50 million, Kamen and his engineering team developed and built the iBot Transporter, a six-wheel robotic wheelchair that could climb stairs and even stand on two wheels so that its occupant could see eye-to-eye with others. To demonstrate the iBot's effectiveness, Kamen once used it to climb the stairs from a Paris Metro station to the restaurant level of the Eiffel Tower. Johnson & Johnson sells the iBot today for approximately $20,000.

In the late 1990s, rumors started to emerge that one of America's greatest inventors had come up with a revolutionary new product idea that had enormous potential. However, no one knew exactly what Kamen was working on, and he was not talking. At a time when

Internet hype seemed to infuse everything connected to technology, speculation in the media included outrageous claims that Kamen had invented a hydrogen-powered hovercraft or an antigravity machine.

Instead, Kamen and the DEKA engineers had conceived of taking the iBot technology to a new level designing a novel, environmentally friendly transportation machine aimed at radically changing how humans get around. Kamen called it the Segway Human Transporter. Using advanced microelectronics, sensors, motors, and gyroscopes, he and his team of engineers built a self-balancing, two-wheeled, electric-powered, motorized scooter. The Segway could travel at about twelve miles per hour, and the rider could change direction solely by leaning forward or backward and using the handlebars to turn left or right. To stop, all the rider had to do was to shift their weight to the center; the machine had no separate braking system. Segway was ergonomically packaged with forged steel and special tires, weighing in at eighty pounds with a travel range of fifteen miles. Kamen expected his transporter to retail for $5,000.

Kamen saw huge volume potential for his product in a world concerned about rising oil prices, increased air and noise pollution, climate change, and urban congestion. He was so excited by the possibilities that instead of staying within the boundaries of DEKA's traditional royalty revenue model and licensing the technology to a large corporation to manufacture and market, he decided to establish his own dedicated organization to commercialize Segway. He planned to hire the people, build the factories to make the machines, develop marketing plans, recruit a sales force, and establish a dealer network around the world. Target markets included pedestrians, postal deliverymen, college students moving around campuses, warehouse employees, police forces, retail mall and theme park workers, and soldiers. Kamen envisioned a multibillion dollar a year opportunity and was anxious to go after it.

Since no one understood Segway's technology or its market potential better than Dean Kamen, he concluded that he should run the company. However, his tendency toward secrecy made it very difficult to recruit experienced transportation and manufacturing executives to New Hampshire to oversee the specific operations required to actually mass produce and sell Segways. Given his expectation that the product would sell several hundred thousand units in its inaugural year, ramping up to over 22 million units annually by year ten, Kamen wanted a team from big, well-established companies that had experience with large-scale global operations. The recruiting challenge facing Kamen was magnified because many people considered him a self-centered control freak. As Kamen himself said, "My own father, who I assume likes me, has referred to me as a human irritant."[1]

Nonetheless, he hired experienced corporate executives from Chrysler and Proctor & Gamble into senior management roles. The capital needed to finance the ramp-up of facilities, inventory, and personnel exceeded what Kamen was personally comfortable supporting. For the first time he had to find outside financing partners. Fortunately, it was 1999 during the Internet boom when the $50 million of venture capital he desired seemed readily available. Kamen proved up to the fund-raising challenge using his outstanding sales skills, passion, and enthusiasm to describe a business that had the potential within five years to reach over $25 billion in value, and tripling from there in the next five years.

Kamen secured an audience with one of Silicon Valley's best known, most highly-respected venture capitalist, John Doerr of Kleiner, Perkins, Caulfield & Byers. Doerr was a legend, having backed and worked with numerous iconic start-up companies including Netscape, Amazon.com, and Google. He was a rock star often acting as the industry's spokesman on national policy issues surrounding technology and entrepreneurship. Doerr signed on and added his own promotional weight to the secretive project further fueling the media frenzy even by suggesting that Kamen's new company would reach $1 billion in revenue faster than any company in history. Kamen successfully raised $90 million of equity financing for Segway behind the leadership of Kleiner Perkins and funds managed by Credit Suisse First Boston, and maintained a personal controlling interest in the company.

Kamen introduced Segway to the world on ABC's *Good Morning America* on December 3, 2001, proclaiming, "If this thing has the kind of impact we're hoping for, cities will become pedestrian-only." Kamen and his team were ready to ramp up production and begin to distribute their new product. Their new factory had the capacity to produce up to 40,000 Segways each month.

However, less than two years later, the U.S. Consumer Product Safety Commission announced that Segway had recalled all 6,000 of its human transporters, a number well-below Kamen's early volume projections, because of reports of a falling hazard, although there had been only three reports of injury. The problem was believed to be caused when the batteries ran low and ceased generating sufficient power to keep the machine upright. Undeterred, in 2004 Kamen raised an incremental $31 million of equity from wealthy individuals to support the growth and development of the business. However, in September 2006, the U.S. Consumer Product Safety Commission announced another Segway recall, this time of 23,500 electric scooters, because of a risk that the machine could unexpectedly apply reverse torque to the wheels, causing the rider to fall. After the second recall, sales tapered off. The Segway never achieved the stellar growth projected by Dean Kamen and John Doerr, and failed to generate any profits. The company became a high-profile white elephant, and with the very quiet sale of the company to a British business magnate[2] in December 2009 for an undisclosed sum, Kamen's dream of turning Segway into the urban transportation medium of the future ended.

What went wrong? Here was an experienced entrepreneur with a long track record of success. Kamen's human transporter was ingenious; a technology breakthrough of a magnitude rarely seen. Kamen had access to plenty of capital to support a ramp-up in operations, and had received an overwhelming amount of free publicity and buzz surrounding the launch. Segway had financial support and backing from very experienced investors including one of the most successful venture capitalists in the United States. It wasn't enough.

DEKA had never conducted any market research to test demand for the product. Kamen was afraid of letting the world in on his great invention too early, and the team loved the pre-announcement mystery and hype, which generated a level of excitement that would have been lost had word gotten out too early. Most consumer product companies would cite this omission as a classic misstep. But many terrific products that exceed the boundaries of our imagination would never get strong feedback from a focus group or market survey. If you tried the product, as did Steve Jobs and Jeff Bezos, both of whom thought it interesting but not worth investing in, you might be wowed, finding it clever and fun; but this is not the same as finding it useful or worth paying $5,000 to own. Nor is it the same when municipal regulations constrain where riders can use the product, when wearing a helmet doesn't make an attractive fashion statement for everyday users, or when the product's weight makes it unwieldy, especially for smaller people. Many consumer products falter when their complexity leads to a product recall that undermines market perception and increases the natural resistance of consumers to buying something new. Kamen endowed Segway with many positive attributes, but not enough to break through and claim commercial success.

*   *   *

As Dean Kamen learned, bringing new, leading-edge technology to market can be very tricky in the transportation sector with its myriad regulations, mechanical challenges, and large capital needs. Doing so with novice management adds to the challenge.

It is a common perception that experienced executives from large corporations with substantial business training, a broad base of contacts, and plentiful scars from past mistakes have a significant advantage over young upstarts. But, the skills required to lead an early-stage venture are different. The managerial attributes needed to scale the corporate ladder often are not required by a resource-starved new company which feeds on creativity, self-reliance, perseverance, and passion.

CHARISMA INCARNATE

He was handsome and flamboyant, a jet-setter married to a super-model and a part-owner of the New York Yankees and the San Diego Chargers. He set up headquarters for his new company on the forty-third floor of a glass and steel skyscraper on Park Avenue in New York City. John DeLorean had style, courage, and ego and over twenty years of car-making experience; everything one needs to launch a new automobile company. Well, almost everything.

Born to a working class family in Detroit, John DeLorean was raised during the Great Depression. A good student in high school, three years' service in the Army during World War II, and a college degree positioned him well to participate in the postwar industrial boom. After completing a graduate degree in automotive engineering from the Chrysler Institute, DeLorean landed at Packard Motors, quickly rising to become the head of research on the back of a creative design for a new transmission for which he was awarded twelve patents.

In 1955, the Pontiac Division of General Motors recruited DeLorean to help the company reposition the storied brand for a less-stodgy demographic. At age thirty-six the hard-charging DeLorean received a significant promotion becoming Pontiac's chief engineer responsible for new product development. In this new capacity he helped manage the creation and launch of a new, two-seat sports car, the Pontiac

GTO. Before that, Pontiac had had a pedestrian image, but DeLorean showed his flair for styling with the GTO, ushering in the era of the "muscle car," a fast and flashy vehicle targeting a younger customer group. Expected to sell 5,000 units annually, the GTO became a huge winner for GM selling 250,000 vehicles in its first five years. Based on this success, DeLorean was again promoted, becoming the general manager of Pontiac in 1965. At age forty, DeLorean had become the youngest division general manager in the history of General Motors. He was on the leadership fast track in America's largest and most significant industrial enterprise.

DeLorean's meteoric rise continued. Four years later he won the top spot at GM's largest division, Chevrolet. Executive status, coming with a big salary and bigger bonuses, fit DeLorean. He decided that his personal life needed improvement as well, and he divorced his wife, had plastic surgery to smooth out his jaw, and upgraded his wardrobe. The engineering-trained DeLorean found that the marketing and advertising aspects of the car business had more appeal, often placing him in Southern California for business. In Hollywood he took advantage of his new "good looks" to date celebrities. He eventually married an aspiring actress.

When DeLorean was promoted again in 1972, becoming vice president in charge of all GM's car and truck production and getting an office on the executive floor at its Detroit headquarters, it was clear that he was on his way to becoming the leader of the company. He also decided to get a new wife, this time marrying supermodel Christina Ferrare. Compared to the staid corporate image of the Detroit automobile executive living in the plush suburbs of Grosse Pointe, DeLorean enjoyed living in the fast lane. But, one year later, at age forty-eight, with the corner office in sight, DeLorean shocked the business community when he abruptly quit GM. He had had enough of corporate America. Instead of jumping to a competitor or large automotive supplier DeLorean became president of the National Alliance of Businessmen, a nonprofit enterprise founded by Lyndon Johnson and Henry Ford II to provide assistance to needy Americans. He also co-wrote a best-selling book, *On a Clear Day You Can See General Motors*, describing his experiences at GM and portraying the company in a negative light.

In 1975 DeLorean announced that he was reentering the car business, but this time as an entrepreneur attempting the unthinkable: starting a new automobile company. A new car company had not succeeded in America in over twenty-five years, but DeLorean thought he could pull it off. After all, he knew as much as anybody how to design, build, and market automobiles; he had managerial talent and access to many wealthy people who could fund his dream. But if starting a new company has lots of hurdles, trying to succeed in a mature industry with considerable capital intensity and fierce competition ranks near the top of all business challenges. In the late 1940s, Preston Tucker had pulled together a unique automobile design with fancy styling, advanced safety features, and an unconventional rear-mounted engine in a high-profile attempt to break into the business. Tucker raised millions of dollars in a public offering, sold dealerships and logo items even before he had a car ready for the road, won the big prize of getting a huge former aircraft engine manufacturing site for his production at a nominal cost from the U.S. government, and rose to national prominence on top of a countrywide publicity campaign. It didn't matter. After producing approximately forty-eight cars, mostly hand-crafted, Tucker shut down operations, having run out of money, amid lawsuits, allegations, and scandals that had undermined his bold effort.[3]

DeLorean was not deterred. He quickly recruited several experienced managers from other companies and incorporated his new enterprise— DeLorean Motor Company (DMC). DeLorean knew that a new car company could not attempt to enter the mainstream market from a raw start unless it had massive financial backing and a well-honed manufacturing and distribution base. The key to his plan was to design a high-end sports car, something that befit his personal self-image, with advanced styling and novel safety features. He based his strategy on targeting a relatively small, but highly lucrative niche market segment, going after the Chevrolet Corvette, which had become dated, and Porsche customers. As with Tucker's approach twenty-five years earlier, DeLorean's first step was to try to capture attention with distinctive styling. He recruited one of the foremost Italian car designers to lead the effort to create his inaugural vehicle, the DMC-12. DeLorean's goal was to bring to market a luxurious two-passenger sports car made with gull-wing doors, four-wheel independent suspension, and a four-speed manual or a three-speed automatic transmission. It would be constructed of a molded-fiberglass reinforced plastic compound with an outer skin of brushed stainless steel to avoid rust and corrosion. It also was to come with a passive restraint system for both driver and passenger, four-wheel disc brakes, and a fuel cell located in the center part of the underbody to place it at a maximum distance from the perimeter of the vehicle. The DMC-12's initial expected sticker price was $12,500.

Using $700,000 of his own money to seed the business DeLorean quickly raised another $12 million from his network of wealthy friends and celebrities—including Johnny Carson and Sammy Davis, Jr.—and sold $10 million of dealership rights in advance of production. DeLorean's objective of manufacturing 30,000 vehicles a year seemed manageable given that the U.S. sports car market totaled approximately 800,000 automobiles annually. However, building and selling, distributing and servicing even one hundred cars a day would not be easy.

Even if he had caught robust economic tailwinds DeLorean's task was risky. In 1973, at the beginning of a worldwide recession and staggering inflation rates resulting from OPEC's push on oil prices, it became daunting. However, DeLorean recognized that his venture had a huge asset in a recession: it would create jobs. He decided to auction off the employment opportunities from opening up an automobile assembly plant, finding interest in Puerto Rico and Northern Ireland. In fact, the United Kingdom was so anxious to generate employment in Northern Ireland—where the government faced civil unrest in West Belfast and one-third of the workforce was unemployed—that it bid aggressively for this opportunity to create several thousand new jobs, despite an external consultant's report stating that DeLorean's company had only a 10 percent chance of success. The British government won the day, offering DMC $135 million in loans and loan guarantees.

With financing in place and an exciting new vehicle design, DMC began constructing the six-building, 660,000-square-foot manufacturing facility in October 1978. The plan was to produce 20,000 cars the first year, rolling the initial vehicles off the assembly line in late 1979. Unfortunately, early in the process of moving the car from the concept to production, DeLorean, a highly experienced automotive engineer, found that they had to make major changes in the car's design due to difficulties in sourcing parts and meeting specifications, and cost changes. The DMC-12 ended up using a lower-performing Renault engine, which took ten seconds (versus an expected eight and a half seconds) to reach sixty miles an hour, and a sporty Lotus Esprit design with a stainless steel body attached. In the end, the car that DeLorean expected to sell for $12,500 would cost twice as much, exceeding the sticker price of a Porsche 924 by 15 percent and the Corvette's price by 50 percent.

Not surprisingly, as with any new car, much less one from an untested organization, the DMC-12 encountered significant design and assembly problems. One problem was that the door panels did not sit flush with the car body, which forced the company to rebuild by hand most of the vehicles when they arrived in the United States from Northern Ireland. Other problems emerged as well. For example, although the stainless-steel outer body panels protected against rust and corrosion, they showed dirt and dust and all kinds of markings, including fingerprints, spoiling some of the car's allure.

Despite slick advertising, a national dealer network, and tremendous free publicity, demand for the DMC-12 fell far short of DeLorean's early projections. The $25,000 sticker price in a difficult economy put huge sales pressure on DMC. Even long-established car models with price tags exceeding $10,000 never had annual sales above 20,000 units. With financial breakeven at 10,000 vehicles per year, DMC saw trouble ahead. However, DeLorean remained undaunted, and by December 1981 the West Belfast plant had built nearly 7,000 cars, although DeLorean had sold only 3,000 units. To keep the British government happy, DeLorean had broken a cardinal automobile industry rule: he was producing cars to fit the manufacturing model instead of meeting dealer orders. DMC was running out of cash. Wall Street underwriters told DeLorean that they would not try to raise money in an IPO unless the factory could produce one hundred cars a day. Company viability became a problem, and U.S. Securities and Exchange Commission (SEC) concerns forced DMC to cancel a $27 million IPO in January 1982. The British government declined to provide incremental funding, and DMC was forced to lay off 1,100 Irish workers, letting the remaining 1,300 employees go only five months later.

Sometimes desperate people do desperate things. To have any chance of saving his company, DeLorean needed more money fast. In a last-ditch effort to raise over $20 million in new capital, DeLorean got himself involved in a cocaine smuggling scheme in late 1982. The operation turned out to be an FBI setup, and the U.S. Drug Enforcement Administration caught DeLorean on videotape in a highly publicized sting operation.

Soon thereafter DeLorean Motor Company ran out of options and filed for bankruptcy. A federal judge acquitted John DeLorean of all charges in 1984, concluding that the U.S. law enforcement agencies had acted inappropriately. When asked by reporters if he planned to get back into the car business, DeLorean replied, "Would you buy a used car from me?"

DMC failed for numerous reasons, including insufficient resources given the dimensions of what DeLorean tried to achieve, poor execution in the design, manufacturing and financing problems, unfortunate timing given what was happening in the U.S. economy as the DMC-12 was coming to market, and targeting too small a market niche with a product that was too expensive. One might expect that an experienced automotive executive like DeLorean would know how to fit together these pieces of the puzzle. Although he got many things right, he did not get enough of them correct to turn his vision into a reality.

Starting an automobile company from the ground up may be among the most challenging of all new ventures. Will the new car companies forming today seeking to take advantage of the perceived opportunity around electric and hybrid vehicles learn from the mistakes of DeLorean and Tucker—by raising sufficient capital, developing the quality product and cost structure to survive, establishing a large enough dealer network, eluding product recalls, scaling their manufacturing operations appropriately, building cars with enough distinctiveness to stand out from the constant flow of new offerings of the more established global manufacturers and the other aggressive and creative start-ups, having the opportunity to take advantage of escalating oil prices, and avoiding macroeconomic pressures that could curb demand? The road map of past mistakes should help.

*   *   *

Unfortunately, the inventory of highly visible, expensive, start-up companies that never reach sustained profitability overwhelms the success stories. The difference between making it through the pass and falling short often comes down to a few poor management decisions, inadequate planning, unanticipated surprises, or an empty bank account. Sometimes management inexperience explains the shortfall, but even those with years of relevant background and responsibility, such as Kamen and DeLorean, often do not comprehend the difficulties of successfully launching a new enterprise. However, new ventures are tricky to pull off in the first place, reminding us of how impressive the achievements are when the enterprise succeeds.

CHAPTER 7

BAD BOYS

Character is much easier kept than recovered.
—Thomas Paine

THE BUSINESS WORLD HAS AN UNSAVORY SIDE, ONE THAT supports the public's image of businesspeople as greedy and unethical. While these qualities are hardly the exclusive province of the business community, daily headlines in the media chronicle the missteps, misbehavior, and wrongdoing of many players. Entrepreneurs are mostly known as hard-charging, "take no prisoners," "eat their young," action-oriented individuals. No one ever says that they are virtuous. The most successful company founders aren't guaranteed entrance through the pearly gates. Sadly, even when their gambles succeed some entrepreneurs misplace their bearings, cut corners, and lose perspective, breaking the rules with the hope and expectation that their company might go further, faster, and become more profitable. While it is often unclear whether they expect to get away with their transgressions, the quest sometimes suspends common sense, the fear of losing trumps their better judgment, or the publicity surrounding their success becomes so addictive that they can't stand not being in the limelight. While most entrepreneurs stop when they get to the edge, some cross over the line of permissibility. When they do, the end result is not pretty, as federal prosecutors orchestrate public perp walks, the lawyers ramp up, and some great innovative businesses melt away beneath headlines of misdeeds. It may not be fair to lump white collar criminals, a la Bernie Madoff and Charles Ponzi, with the entrepreneur who gets carried away and pushes beyond acceptable boundaries, but that distinction falls outside this message. Innovators don't deserve a free pass, but, every so often, their ingenuity, determination, and resolve alters an industry.

*　*　*

In *The Tempest*, William Shakespeare wrote, "What is past is prologue." Wall Street has proved him very prescient. Long before the 2008 collapse of Lehman Brothers and Bear Stearns, there was Drexel Burnham Lambert. Long before Rudy Giuliani became mayor of New York City and a candidate for the U.S. presidency, there was Drexel Burnham Lambert. Long before the world focused on subprime mortgages, credit default swaps, and overflowing hedge fund coffers, there was Drexel Burnham Lambert. There was a time, not that long ago, when the true epicenter of the financial universe was not London, Tokyo, Hong Kong, Frankfurt or New York, but at the intersection of Rodeo Drive and Wilshire Boulevard in Beverly Hills, California. That's where you found Michael Milken, senior vice president of Drexel Burnham Lambert.

IN THE BEGINNING

Investment bankers have been around for hundreds of years, practicing a profession that rewards the movement of money, especially a lot of money. Investment bankers learned long ago they can earn sizable amounts for themselves when their clients willingly pay a small percentage commission for services rendered. Those employed on Wall Street, in the City of London, and in and around numerous bourses throughout the world understand that they have the opportunity to generate substantial personal wealth solely by taking an apparently thin slice of each financing pie that comes by. Over the years, the bankers have maintained a relatively similar-sized percentage, but the pies have gotten bigger, leaving them with more valuable slices as well. Unfortunately for some, the prospect of big bonuses and large capital gains interferes with serving their clients and begets unethical behavior. We have seen it often enough.

Growing up in a middle-class neighborhood in suburban Los Angeles, Michael Milken had an uneventful childhood. He went north for college, graduating in 1968 from the University of California, Berkeley, summa cum laude and Phi Beta Kappa. While the late 1960s brought tremendous turmoil and chaos to American cities with riots and Vietnam War protests ushering in a more liberal social agenda, Milken opted for an unfashionable career—business. Traveling back East to the University of Pennsylvania's famed Wharton School, he gained an MBA. In 1970, after graduation, Milken joined the Philadelphia office of a relatively small but long-standing financial firm, Drexel Harriman Ripley, where he researched bonds and looked for attractive values. Drexel lacked the prestige of the more well-known Wall Street firms of the day, such as Morgan Stanley, Kuhn Loeb, Dillon Read, Goldman Sachs, and First Boston. It earned its money on the fringes serving smaller companies and investors.

In college Milken had read a study from the 1950s showing that during the first half of the twentieth century, a broad portfolio of bonds issued by non–Blue Chip companies provided a higher rate of return than a diversified group of bonds that had been issued by high-quality companies. In other words, the lower grade companies paid higher rates of interest to entice investors to lend them money, but the rate of default on these "noninvestment grade" bonds was not that much higher. Milken had identified an attractive mismatch in the perceived risk of owning these bonds versus the prospective reward. Through his position at Drexel he had the means to capture the value. In the 1970s, the market for these types of bonds was small, but Milken saw an opportunity to create more liquidity by buying and selling these securities to financial institutions, such as insurance companies and pension funds. He concluded that he could generate tidy profits for Drexel by recommending that its clients buy these non-investment-grade bonds. He moved his office to New York to better capitalize on this idea. Milken was convinced that his insight would lead to higher rates of return for bond holders, but the investment strategy was risky and required superb salesmanship to bond portfolio managers, who only wanted to purchase highly-rated bonds and who distrusted anything other than investment-grade securities. Up to the challenge and passionate about the opportunity, Milken developed a detailed understanding of these less well-rated bonds and the companies that had issued them. As he expanded the market for these bonds, trading volume picked up, enabling Milken to begin to generate substantial profits for Drexel (now renamed Drexel Burnham Lambert). Eventually, he persuaded his boss to allow him to further increase the firm's sales and trading activity. In 1973, his trading positions produced an amazing 100 percent rate of return. Not surprisingly, he got more capital to risk to build his inventory of bonds, and for 1974 the rate of return totaled an impressive 40 percent. With such substantial profits, Milken began to make a name for himself within Drexel, and also with those delighted clients who had bought into his strategy and were earning higher yields on their bond portfolios.

Milken was on his way to greatness, creating innovation in the financial sector. There may not be a better example in the business world of a person so significantly recasting the company he joined fresh out of business school. Identifying a new business opportunity and then implementing it successfully inside a well-established company does not happen often. It takes many of the same skills and passion that entrepreneurs employ in start-up companies. The accomplishment speaks volumes about the capabilities of the person, the flexibility of the organization and its incumbent leadership, and the innovativeness of the idea. Although Drexel was buffeted by many of the trends afflicting Wall Street at that time, perhaps making it more open to something new, Milken's unique talents and strong conviction that his insights were correct laid the foundation for entrepreneurial excellence.

LET THE GOOD TIMES ROLL

When the U.S. economy faltered in the mid-1970s recession, some companies that had sold bonds in healthier economic times found that their businesses were distressed. The price of their bonds fell, increasing their yields and creating a larger inventory for Milken and his team to trade. In the financial world additional activity tends to be good for salesmen and traders who love the extra liquidity and the opportunity to earn more fees and commissions. Milken was no different. If "some" was good, "more" was better.

At the time U.S. Treasury bonds offered annual returns of about 7.5 percent, but Milken's higher-yielding bonds earned double-digit returns. Demand for these high-yield, or "junk," bonds continued to grow as more and more institutions realized that Milken had correctly predicted low default rates despite paying high interest. Plus, a bigger market meant a more liquid market, which made it easier for buyers and sellers to transact. Of course, as the placement agent, Milken knew who owned all these bonds and who wanted to buy more. Drexel even created and sold mutual funds solely to own high-yield bonds, enlarging the market opportunity so that smaller investors could play alongside the big financial institutions.

By the late 1970s, Drexel's business was picking up real momentum, requiring Milken to spend more and more time on management activities that distracted him from his primary pursuit of selling high-yield bonds. Increasingly desirous of having his own space away from the investment bankers seemingly taking over the firm in New York, and perhaps hoping to avoid the oversight that inevitably comes when the money at risk escalates, Milken took a bold action that was possible only because of the huge percentage of the firm's profits that he generated. He announced that he was returning to his roots and moving his entire team of junk bond salesmen and traders across the country to Southern California. To gain more family time, Milken worked East Coast hours, starting each day at 4:30 AM. On his desk, he had a sign that read, "The harder I work the luckier I get."[1] No one worked harder or was a more persuasive salesman than Michael Milken. No one was more knowledgeable about the companies Wall Street financed than Michael Milken. No one was more driven to create and command a market than Michael Milken. As his business grew and the profits gushed forth he became *the* rock star of the financial world. And, there was more to come, much more.

With its unique capability to sell high-yield bonds for smaller companies Drexel attracted entrepreneurs seeking access to growth capital. Among the most tenacious was Steve Wynn, who oversaw a small Las Vegas casino, the Golden Nugget. Wynn had limited profits, but needed $100 million to build a new hotel and casino. Turned down by others, Wynn found a supporter in Milken, who successfully raised the necessary money for this highly risky venture in part by giving bond buyers confidence that Drexel knew what it was doing in underwriting the credit. This successful financing opened the opportunity for other growth companies, including MCI Communications and its long-distance telephone services, Tele-Communications, Inc. and its cable television services, and McCaw Cellular's wireless services, to ramp up growth in their capital intensive businesses. If an entrepreneurial company needed capital and could not get a warm reception from commercial banks, Drexel became an attractive alternative.

In 1980, Drexel's business was accelerating having reached a critical mass of bond issuers and buyers to provide a liquid market of scale. Milken decided to further cement his control of the market by bringing his best customers together and inviting them to Los Angeles to participate in the first High-Yield Bond Conference. It was a simple affair initially. But in the coming years, as the supply and demand of junk bonds ramped up, Milken tapped into Hollywood's flash and fame. He threw dazzling soirees as the sponsor of the most influential networking event on the annual financial community calendar. Each year upward of 2,000 movers and shakers from the corporate and financial worlds congregated at the Beverly Hilton Hotel; the guest list included corporate CEOs, financiers, prominent academic speakers, and A-list celebrity entertainers. Invitation to what became known as "the predator's ball" was highly coveted, as was the opportunity to kiss Milken's ring.

The business kept rolling. In 1981 only five other investment banking firms participated in the high-yield bond business. Drexel's market share stood at 70 percent, but Milken wanted 100 percent of the market. Because it controlled such a substantial portion of the high-yield bond sales and trading activity, Drexel began to insist upon additional compensation for its services, over and above the standard underwriting spread. Arguing that they needed extra incentives to entice bond buyers Milken began demanding detachable warrants from the bond issuers, allowing the bond buyers to acquire shares in the issuing companies. Sometimes, however, Milken kept the warrants for the account of Drexel and its partners, or he sold them separately to third parties, pocketing the value for the firm.

Drexel's investment bankers had found plenty of companies that were desirous of tapping the high-yield bond market, but soon the potential supply of bond issues overwhelmed the investment capacity of bond buyers. The U.S. government, inadvertently, was there to help. To support the American dream of home ownership Congress had established savings and loans companies (S&L's) to provide mortgages. Favorable legislation in the 1960s boosted their prominence. However, in 1980 and 1981 many of the nation's 3,000 S&L's faced significant financial problems because they had violated one of the most basic tenets of finance: they had made long-term, fixed-rate mortgage loans with monies provided through shorter-term passbook and savings accounts. During the 1960s and 1970s, the S&L's had agreed to lend money for long periods of time at between 4 percent and 5 percent interest rates. But, interest rates jumped precipitously to double-digits in 1980, increasing the lenders' cost of money. Without the ability to pass on the added cost, over seven hundred thrift banks failed during the period, creating an approximately $160 billion liability, which

U.S. taxpayers eventually absorbed. In response, and eager to prevent further damage to the country's financial system, lawmakers loosened the rules so that S&L's could improve profitability by moving some of their assets into higher yielding commercial loans and corporate debt securities. Lax federal regulation allowed some of the S&L's to further boost their profits by allowing them to use their low-cost federally-insured funds to buy the riskier, but higher-yielding bonds peddled by Drexel. It did not take long for Milken and his team to find an entirely new group of significant buyers anxious to earn the higher interest rates offered by junk bonds. More buyers broadened the market increasing the firm's profitability and heightening Milken's domination of the high-yield market.

AND THE BAND PLAYED ON

Life got even better for Drexel in the early 1980s when mergers and acquisitions activity in corporate America accelerated. Historically, tax laws allow corporations to deduct interest expense, often making it marginally cheaper for companies to finance with debt versus equity. Although debt comes with repayment obligations, the perception that there is a ready market for refinancing bonds when they become due makes it seem like permanent capital, akin to equity. When the high inflation rates experienced in the 1970s drove up asset values, some companies felt that their share prices were not keeping pace. Undervalued assets plus the availability of debt at a relatively low after-tax cost whetted the appetite of corporate buyers who saw the potential for outsized returns on equity. This confluence of trends was tailor-made for Drexel's investment bankers and Michael Milken's bond salesmen and traders. Since large corporations worked with the mainstream Wall Street firms, Drexel had its investment bankers target a different group of prospective acquirers who could take advantage of the firm's strong high-yield bond placement capability: newly formed investment partnerships focused on leveraged buyouts (LBOs). These firms—including Kohlberg Kravis Roberts and Forstmann Little—specialized in buying control of companies using a small amount of equity and a large amount of borrowed funds secured by the existing assets and supported by the future cash flows of the acquired business. It proved to be a wonderful marriage.

One of the challenges for prospective buyers in hostile takeovers was arranging the financing prior to the initial overture. Not surprisingly, the potential institutional buyers of the acquisition debt would not commit to buy bonds before knowing the details of the contemplated transaction, and to do that they had to sign nondisclosure agreements upfront, which also meant that they had to stop trading in any of the underlying securities. This, they were loathe to do. Milken soon concluded that if his team could raise money for a "friendly acquisition" negotiated between a buyer and seller, they might also finance an unfriendly takeover.

Investment banks could use their own funds to underwrite a portion of a client's proposed takeover transaction in what was called a "bridge loan." But, Drexel, with its relatively small balance sheet was unwilling to take this risk, so they developed an innovative solution that would leverage their strength in the high-yield bond market; they would issue a letter to the relevant parties saying that they were "highly confident" they could raise the money. While this letter was not binding on Drexel, the marketing power and consistent success of the Milken fund-raising machine carried momentous weight and credibility, reducing significantly the risk of actually raising the money. Moreover, Drexel could charge a multimillion dollar fee for issuing a letter, without having to risk any of its own money. It was a brilliant idea that was available only to Drexel because other investment banks did not have the market clout or position to give all the necessary constituencies certainty that the money would show up on time to consummate the transaction. Mostly, though, the other investment banks did not have Michael Milken.

The thesis was simple: entrepreneurial, aggressive, operating companies and financial buyers could, with access to Drexel's financing prowess, become large players in hostile takeovers; "Friends of Mike" could gain access to enormous amounts of buying power. Drexel's acquisitive clients included T. Boone Pickens, whose Mesa Petroleum went after Gulf Oil and Unocal; Ted Turner, who sought CBS and bought MGM/UA; Carl Icahn, who bought TWA and went after Phillips Petroleum; Henry Kravis, whose firm famously purchased RJR Nabisco; Ron Perelman, who used his MacAndrews & Forbes to acquire Revlon; and media baron Rupert Murdoch, whose News Corp. gobbled up numerous newspapers and broadcast properties around the world. Over time Drexel's fundraising capacity proved so powerful that its clients could raise a war chest for prospective acquisitions even prior to identifying specific targets.

Michael Milken had created a new financial ecosystem: first, by providing liquidity to owners of bonds of struggling companies; then by creating a new issue market for high-yield bonds; then by supporting a new universe of buyers of such bonds and connecting all of this from his X-shaped trading desk on the fourth floor of a nondescript building in Beverly Hills. Moreover, Drexel had developed a unique business: it could get paid in multiple ways at near-monopoly rates. Milken had created both the supply and the demand for junk bonds, sitting at the crossroads of a rapidly growing, highly lucrative universe. In 1986 Michael Milken personally earned $714 million from his salary, bonus, and partnership interests.

The commercial banks were lenders in many of Drexel's deals, but their loans were generally short-term and secured. Without Drexel to place the unsecured, subordinated debt, these mergers and acquisitions by smaller companies and financial buyers would never have happened. And while other investment banking firms now were eager to play Drexel's part, these new "megadeals" spawned securities in amounts that no investment banking firm but Drexel had the muscle to sell. Drexel's near monopoly of this market segment, following the earlier years of near-monopoly of the nontakeover junk market, resulted in an unprecedented trajectory of growth on Wall Street. At the end of 1977, the firm had amassed only $150 million in capital with revenues reaching approximately $150 million. By the end of 1985, Drexel's revenues had grown to $2.5 billion and the firm had about $1 billion of capital. By the end of 1986, Drexel's revenues had soared to a record $4 billion and its after-tax earnings reached an estimated $545 million, making it the most profitable investment banking firm in America.

Other investment banks soon wanted a piece of Drexel's action. But, as latecomers to the game, some of these firms placed high-yield debt for clients who defaulted relatively soon thereafter. Moreover, without the credibility to sell "highly confident" letters, these firms had to put their own capital at risk, making "bridge loans" to support potential transactions, expecting to place the bonds at a later date. Unfortunately, when the credit markets turned soft, some of these bonds could not find a home—the "bridge" had become a "pier"—and they were either sold at steep discounts or held on the balance sheet at a substantial loss. Nonetheless, competition began to shrink Drexel's market share. The tide was turning.

GREED ISN'T GOOD

Insider trading has long been a scourge of the investment world, and boom times on Wall Street in the mid-1980s set the stage for a new round of this insidious behavior. The increasing dominance of Milken's franchise in high-yield bonds placed Drexel at the center of mergers and acquisitions activity. What better place to learn about the potential transactions that could quickly increase the share price of companies? Not surprisingly, many of the best and brightest investment bankers from other firms gravitated to Drexel to gain an edge and position themselves to be in the know, and then act on it. Milken, too, enjoyed these heady times, recognizing that what he had created at Drexel was unique, powerful, and tremendously lucrative. He had become the most powerful person in the financial world, but he wanted more. Soon, magazine cover stories that had heralded his unparalleled success were about to chronicle a different tale, one that would shock the financial community.

In May 1986, after only a year at Drexel, a thirty-three-year-old investment banker, Dennis Levine, was arrested and accused by the SEC of illegally buying and selling securities using nonpublic information. Although Levine had started trading on inside information prior to joining Drexel, this did not protect his current employer. With Drexel under the magnifying glass, other improprieties surfaced. The investigation into unsavory Wall Street behavior was led by the ambitious U.S. Attorney for the Southern District of New York, Rudolph Giuliani.

In November 1986, Ivan Boesky, one of Wall Street's best known and most successful arbitrageurs, pleaded guilty to insider trading and agreed to pay a $100 million fine, the largest fine ever. Subsequently, the SEC accused Boesky and Milken of illegally acting in consort regarding the purchase of certain stocks. Soon, Drexel's legal troubles became daily news fodder both in the financial and mainstream press, pushing the firm into the spotlight—a position for which it hadn't the temperament or experience. Although the stock market had performed well for much of the 1980s, the upward trend began to turn down in September 1987. On Monday, October 19— Black Monday—the stock market lost 22 percent of its total value, approximately $500 billion in one day, its worst performance since the crash of October 1929. Although Wall Street's bull run was over, U.S. Attorney Giuliani was only getting started.

In September 1988, Drexel was charged with insider trading, stock manipulation, defrauding clients, and stock parking. Giuliani threatened to indict Drexel under RICO, the Racketeer Influenced and Corrupt Organizations Act, which made companies responsible for illegal acts carried out by their employees. For Drexel, getting a RICO indictment would mean posting a $1 billion performance bond or having all of its assets frozen, which would have significantly reduced the quality of the firm's balance sheet by making all its other unsecured borrowings more junior and also seriously impairing its reputation. Historically, if a Wall Street firm suffers a lack of confidence from those who trade with it, it tends to go out of business very quickly (as was further evidenced by Lehman Brothers and Bear Stearns in 2008). Drexel decided that it had little choice but to fight the charges, since the alternative would have forced it to close.

Shortly after Drexel was charged, news surfaced of a limited partnership, MacPherson Partners, controlled by Michael Milken. To ease the placement of a new issue of high-yield bonds, Drexel often persuaded the issuers to sweeten the potential return for buyers by including warrants to buy shares in the issuer's company. Drexel would sometimes "strip" the warrants from the offering and keep them for its own account or give them to its employees as part of their compensation. Milken's partnership was a repository for some of the warrants Drexel earned from these high-yield bond issues. However, among the limited partners at MacPherson Partners were select, individual money managers who purchased the high-yield bonds for the mutual funds they were responsible for managing. It was not a big leap for prosecutors to see these ownership stakes as bribes to induce the money managers to buy the bonds.

With the threat of RICO and the added evidence of these partnerships, Giuliani forced Drexel to plead guilty to numerous counts of illegal trading activity and stock manipulation, pay $650 million in fines, and compel the removal of Michael Milken from his post at the center of the high-yield bond market. Milken was charged with ninety-six counts of fraud and racketeering, and Drexel became a convicted felon. In April 1990, Michael Milken pled guilty to six counts of securities and reporting violations, paid a $200 million fine, disgorged $400 million of prior income, and was sentenced to ten years in prison. Two years later he was diagnosed with prostate cancer; his sentence was reduced to time served, and he was released.

On top of all the Drexel controversy, further pain came from the collapse of the high-yield bond market in early 1990, precipitated by a new federal law requiring S&Ls to dispose of their junk bonds. Without Michael Milken at the helm, there was no counterbalance to the bad news, and no credible source of support for this market. As the most significant market maker of these instruments, Drexel ran into a liquidity problem when the collateral value of its inventory plunged, forcing the commercial banks to cut off their credit lines to the firm.

Despite its $3.6 billion in gross assets, Drexel filed for protection under the federal bankruptcy laws in February 1990, making for the largest failure on Wall Street until Lehman Brothers went bust in 2008. Nonetheless, Michael Milken's creation of the high-yield bond market had totally transformed global corporate finance, mergers and acquisitions, the leverage buy-out business, and notions of Wall Street compensation. His innovations were tremendously powerful and Drexel's execution of the strategy was brilliant, especially as it evolved over time with the new governmental regulations around S&Ls. Milken took the nugget of a good idea around the positive risk-reward to investors of owning lower-credit-quality bonds, packaged it, sold it, found ways to grow the market while achieving rarely attained levels of profit that he used to reward his team and plow back into the business to support even more growth. As economic and political conditions changed, Milken and his team were sufficiently adroit in exploiting new opportunities; they had a huge competitive advantage because they had the foundation in place—established customer relationships, a growing balance sheet, pockets of friendly buyers, a track record of success, incentivized professionals—and they had the courage to keep going. In the process, Drexel grew to become a powerhouse on Wall Street, forever altering the capital markets. Today, the global high-yield market exceeds $1 trillion, and new issuance has reached $150 to $180 billion in good years.

But, too much of a good thing can cause pain. Despite the intelligence, entrepreneurial skills, hard work, and leadership of Michael

Milken, his overwhelming desire to maintain dominance over the high-yield bond market and remain at the heart of the capital and transactional flows and perhaps to derive even more wealth, drove him and his company over the edge, afoul of the law and into the headlines with televised testimony. He became his generation's poster child for excessive behavior. Sad! Great entrepreneur, wildly innovative, but his obituary will likely start by reminding us that he was a convicted felon.

*   *   *

Far away from the canyons of Wall Street and even farther from the lifestyles of the rich and famous in Beverly Hills, another industry was about to get turned on its head. This time the protagonist was a lowly college student. In 1998 Shawn Fanning, a nineteen-year-old computer science major at Boston's Northeastern University, exploited the full power of the personal computer and the increasing bandwidth and accelerating data flow rates of the late 1990s Internet boom, so that a small group of technically proficient software developers could reshape the music world by making it extremely easy and inexpensive to transfer digital bits of data from one user to another without the permission of the copyright holders. In less than two years, using minimal capital, without any advertising or promotional spend, and a small organization, Fanning's company, Napster, Inc., grew from a dorm room idea to an estimated 58 million worldwide users and was continuing to expand rapidly. Napster was the first enterprise to allow people to easily share their digital music collections with one another via the Internet. It was a fabulous idea for a business, except it had one serious drawback: it circumvented the property protection of the owners of recorded music by allowing free downloading of copyrighted songs by anyone with access to a personal computer and an Internet connection. The owners of those songs became highly perturbed.

THE "ME" GENERATION

In the early 1980s Philips and Sony developed compact discs—CDs—which quickly became the preferred means for consumers to buy, store, and enjoy recorded music. In replacing vinyl as the recording media of choice, the CD ushered in a major shift in the music recording industry by offering higher quality sound in a more convenient package. Music

consumers began to replace their old vinyl LP (long-playing) libraries by purchasing boxed CD anthologies of their favorite artists' work.
A further recording technology advancement came from Germany in
1992 when engineers developed the MP3 format for compressing digital audio files, enabling them to be stored and transmitted easily over
the Internet at near CD-quality sound.

Fanning's college roommate was a big music fan and anxious to
expand his library. As a regular visitor to Internet chat rooms, Fanning
saw frequent sharing of music and files and decided to develop software
for sharing MP3 files over the Internet. To do this required specialized
software that could easily be downloaded; Fanning and several friends
wrote these software programs within a few months. So that users could
find the music they wanted, Fanning also had to create software that
allowed them to search for MP3 files, primarily on other people's personal computers. This was no easy task because most search software
was intended to identify material on websites, not on home-computer
hard drives. By connecting one PC user to another, Fanning was among
the early pioneers of "peer-to-peer" data transfers. At the time most
people assumed that individuals would not want to share their personal
files with strangers, but Fanning disagreed and then proved his point.
He understood that certain segments of the population, such as college students, would not mind, and in fact might desire, access to other
people's files, especially if it meant that they could get music recordings
for free without leaving the comfort of their homes or dorm rooms.
Fanning's software turned each user's computer into a small file server
and then linked them together. Napster software scanned each hard
drive to identify the MP3 files and then catalogued them on a central
server. When a user wanted to download a particular song, the Napster
server connected the two computers and the file was shared.

In May 1999, having dropped out of college to pursue Napster full-
time, Fanning's team wrote the software that forever changed music
publishing's business model. Delivering an early version to his friends,
he told them not to share it with others. Not surprisingly, however,
that is exactly what they did, and within a few days an estimated
3,000 users were sharing music files. Shortly thereafter, with the aid
of his uncle, Fanning incorporated Napster to commercialize his file-
sharing software. By October 1999, Napster had raised $2 million
of venture capital from angel investors. It then moved from Boston

to Silicon Valley and tried to establish itself as a real company with experienced management. Napster's free software program propagated with unprecedented speed, especially around college campuses, where students had access to high-speed Internet service and little compulsion to pay for recorded music.

Other music file-sharing services sprouted up providing similar capabilities but utilizing different system architectures, and in some cases, sidestepping the legal storm that later engulfed Napster. In early 2000, Nullsoft, a division of AOL, launched Gnutella, a comparable service that did not use a central file server, instead allowing users to search for and download music files directly from other personal computers. Kazaa, Morpheus, Grokster and others created advertising-related revenue models by launching adware whenever a user accessed their file-sharing services. Napster's explosive growth on campuses quickly overwhelmed many university computer networks, clogging up transmissions. Oregon State University found that 10 percent of the school's bandwidth was occupied by Napster. At Florida State University, Napster was using 20 percent of the bandwidth. The University of Illinois thought their percentage was even higher.

Like information accessed over the Internet, all this music was free. Users had gotten used to, and in fact expected, free Internet content of any and all kinds. The notion that copyrighted music transferred from someone else's computer without payment to the owner amounted to theft of intellectual property either did not occur to, or was not respected by, Napster's growing user population. Napster provided free delivery of an enormous catalog of high-quality music very simply and quickly from anywhere in the world to anyone with an Internet connection. Some people justified their piracy actions, arguing that people could share their CDs or could burn an unlimited number of copies on their home computer's read/write CD drive without any compensation to the copyright holder. Why was this different? Napster argued that it was not violating any copyright laws because it was not hosting the music on its servers, it was only providing a connection between users, peer-to-peer.

By mid-2000 Napster had 3 million users a day, rivaling the number of AOL subscribers, then the leading internet service provider (ISP). In April 2000, the heavy metal rock band Metallica sued the University of Southern California, Yale, Indiana University, and Napster alleging that allowing students to download music over their networks violated the same RICO statutes that Rudolph Giuliani had used in his prosecution of Michael Milken and Drexel Burnham Lambert.[2] Eventually, over two hundred colleges and universities banned the use of Napster over their computer networks, but many other schools, some citing freedom of speech protections under the U.S. Constitution, continued to allow the service even though it was eating up their network bandwidth.

Napster's proliferation threatened the $13 billion per year recording industry—from artists to publishers to retailers. Record labels and their recording artists had a well-worn, if not entirely balanced, business relationship. In exchange for promotion, production, and distribution the Big Five—Sony Music Entertainment, Bertelsmann Music Group, Warner Music, EMI, and Universal Music Group—paid singers, song writers, and musicians for their work. Superstars were paid big money but also generated substantial profits for their music publishers. The record labels had huge infrastructures and fixed costs, including upfront contracts with recording artists. Loss of the marginal sale because of the piracy so easily attainable through Napster and others caused tremendous consternation among industry executives. As with many entrenched companies under attack from new technologies and new competition, they felt that they had to do something to protect themselves and their franchises against this insidious virus-like innovation of users transferring their music without any payments to the copyright owners. They chose a particularly American tactic: they hired lawyers. In December 1999, the music industry's trade association, the Recording Industry Association of America, sued Napster, alleging that it was aiding and abetting massive copyright infringement.

In May 2000, against the backdrop of the stock market's rapidly deflating Internet bubble Napster successfully raised $15 million of equity capital from well-respected Silicon Valley venture capitalists and used the funds to support the growth of the enterprise, recruit experienced management from the recording industry, and pay for an increasingly large legal bill. To protect itself against a growing number of lawsuits, Napster hired famed litigator David Boies to argue their defense. Boies was a celebrity in the legal world for his successful antitrust defense of IBM in the 1970s, and then for representing the U.S. Department of Justice in its antitrust case against Microsoft in 2000, and more recently, for representing Vice President Al Gore in front of the U.S. Supreme

Court in *Gore v. Bush* following the 2000 presidential election. Three fundamental precepts anchored Napster's legal defense. First, the Audio Home Recording Act of 1992 had made sharing music legal for consumers as long as they were not engaged in profit-making. Second, there were plenty of legitimate uses for Napster-based file sharing other than downloading music. Third, as an ISP Napster should not be held liable for listings that appeared in its directory. Napster believed that it served only as a facilitator of communications between personal computers and that because it did not copy files, provide the technology for copying files, compress files, or transfer files it was not in violation of any laws.

Although Napster was held liable for knowingly encouraging and assisting copyright infringement in February 2001 by the California Court of Appeals, the company had demonstrated how to harness the power of the Internet to totally disrupt well-established business models and industry structures, especially when the primary content of products and services was already available in digital form. In the process, it transformed how people all over the world interacted, created, disseminated, and paid for (or not) information that could be digitized. The initial focus was music, but the same challenges existed for other copyrighted material, including books, photographs, films, and videogames. At its peak, in March 2001, Napster's servers were enabling users to copy more than 165 million music files per day.

The company filed for protection under the bankruptcy code in June 2002. Piracy did not pay. In standard early Internet-company fashion, Napster did not survive long enough to generate significant revenue. Distracted early on by intense legal battles, the company never had the time to develop or execute a successful business model. However, a poor college student had ushered in a new world around all things "digitizable." Fanning had no business education, a limited background in computer science, and negligible managerial talent, but these were no longer the prerequisite skills necessary to disrupt a well-established industry. New technology had, once again, caught up with old style business models and paved the way for innovative entrepreneurs to revamp, reconstruct, and revolutionize.

*   *   *

Entrepreneurs are well-known for pushing the envelope but not always knowing where to draw the line and stop. Ethical conduct rules most of the time. On occasion, though, the temptation of greatness or greed takes over. Whereas Michael Milken ultimately used his innovations in junk bonds and high finance to steal from the buyers and sellers of securities, Shawn Fanning's new venture exploited the latest in communications and software technology to steal from the recording artists, music publishing companies, and music retailers. In both cases the entrepreneurs permanently altered their industries, but in the process they ran outside the lines, their companies went bust, and their legacies as movers and shakers will always carry the notation that they had cheated.

CHAPTER 8

ENTERPRISING ENTERPRISES

I was seldom able to see an opportunity until it had ceased to be one.
—Mark Twain

BACK IN 1876, WESTERN UNION, THEN ONE OF THE leading companies in the world with an extensive U.S. telegraph network, got the chance to acquire the key patents behind Alexander Graham Bell's "speaking telegraph." However, because of a combination of corporate arrogance, head-in-the-sand engineering bias, and a real failure to see what might be, the dominant "communications" company of its day evaluated the opportunity and concluded in a now famous internal memo that "this 'telephone' has too many shortcomings to be seriously considered as a means of communication. The device is inherently of no value to us."[1] Initially, Western Union saw the telephone as a toy, not as a potential next wave in communications, because it was too busy enjoying the near-monopoly status of its existing nationwide telegraphy business. The following year the company recognized its error and had to pay a steep price to try to get back in the game accessing telephone technology developed by Thomas Edison.

David Sarnoff, the driving force and entrepreneurial energy behind the stupendous growth and achievements of Radio Corporation of America (RCA), wrote a memo to a corporate vice president in 1915 when he was a young employee at its predecessor company, Marconi Wireless Telegraph Company. It was a time when radio was used primarily for wireless point-to-point communications, such as ship to shore. Sarnoff had a far-reaching vision. He saw the potential to harness existing radio technology and use it for entertainment and information purposes as a broadcasting technique. He proposed that his company manufacture "radio music boxes" for sale to homes and then transmit music programs, baseball box scores, lectures, and news stories to these households. This was the beginning of mass media and entertainment. Having demonstrated great market prescience and capability by launching the radio age, it is surprising that when in 1939 that same David Sarnoff, now a media mogul, introduced television to the public at the New York World's Fair. He was convinced that this new device would change the world, proclaiming: "Now we add sight to sound. It is with a feeling of humbleness that I come to this moment of announcing the birth...of a new art so important in its implications that it is bound to affect all society." The following day the *New York Times* wrote: "The problem with television is that people must sit and keep their eyes glued to the screen; the average American family hasn't time for it...for this reason, if no other, television will never be a serious competitor of [radio] broadcasting."[2] The *New York Times* did not get it, but fortunately the entrepreneurial leader of RCA did.

David Sarnoff and RCA led the way in bringing television to the world, but there are too few examples of established companies developing fresh business models or introducing truly transformative product lines. Maybe it is because they get grounded in the status quo and cannot envision a different landscape, the impact of modern technologies, or changing market conditions. Or maybe it is because they have existing businesses to protect, current cash flow streams that need to grow, and employees that expect a regular paycheck and maybe even a bonus that could be jeopardized by stepping too far out on the limb, despite knowing that it is out on the limb that you find the fruit. Most large companies never figure out how to work outside of their conventional organizations, think of their customers in different ways, or show a willingness to take any meaningful risks. It's not what they do.

Although large companies around the world today are thirsty for innovation, most do not have the culture, leadership, or long-term stamina to make step-function changes in their businesses. Instead, they focus on competing in the current environment and generating near-term profitability. They have not been engineered for continual renewal, bet-the-company, entrepreneurial risk-taking. Only a few have the confidence to risk making mistakes in quest for something unique and better. Apple presents the best example today of a large company with an ingrained culture that demonstrates repeatable innovation, most likely because of the long leadership of its founder/ entrepreneur who had the courage to start with a blank sheet of paper in pursuit of a vision. Steve Jobs experienced firsthand the creation of an innovative company. Apple also operates within an industry so fast-paced and dynamic that it can easily imagine how painful it would be to fall behind the technology curve; a treadmill that seems to accelerate every year.

A LEGACY OF INNOVATION

Modern business mythology often references the Xerox Corporation's inability to capture the personal computer market in the 1970s and 1980s as the classic example of how a big company lost an opportunity. Steve Jobs famously said, "They just grabbed defeat from the greatest victory in the computer industry. Xerox could have owned the entire computer industry today."[3] Maybe not. Commercializing technology, not inventing technology, is fundamental to innovation. Xerox proved great at the former, but it lacked the capabilities for the latter. However, what makes the Xerox story so remarkable is that the company was one of the greatest examples ever of what can be accomplished through applying inventive technology and executing an innovative business model. It created one of the most dominant and profitable businesses ever: plain-paper copying.

After completing a physics degree at the California Institute of Technology in 1930, Chester Carlson trained as an engineer at Bell Laboratories before taking a job at a small electronics firm. Carlson observed, "In the course of my patent work I frequently had a need for copies of patent specifications and drawings, and there was no really convenient way of getting them at that time."[4] Copies were only available at great expense from outside vendors with photostat machines, so Carlson decided to invent his own office copier. After developing an early prototype in 1938, Carlson progressed the technology rapidly, and on April 4, 1939, he filed a patent for a new invention that he called "electrophotography." For the next five years Carlson worked to improve his invention, seeking corporate support from leading U.S. technology companies including IBM, RCA, and General Electric. They showed no interest. In 1944 Carlson finally persevered raising $3,000 from the Battelle Memorial Institute, a private research foundation in Columbus, Ohio, but had to give up 75 percent of any future royalties on his technology. Carlson moved to Columbus to pursue his dream, but his wife thought he was crazy and divorced him.

In 1945, the Haloid Company, a relatively small distributor of photographic paper and supplies in Rochester, New York—the hometown of Eastman Kodak—learned of Carlson's embryonic technology and agreed to fund Battelle's research in exchange for manufacturing rights. Four stressful years later Haloid brought the first plain-paper copier to the market, but it proved too big and heavy, and it required a dedicated highly-skilled operator to make the copies. The product achieved only limited success. Joe Wilson, Haloid's CEO, showed tremendous perseverance, however, funding ten more years of development work and almost bankrupting Haloid in the process, to create a machine that could easily make plain-paper copies. Believing he needed a joint venture partner to market their exciting new product, Wilson approached IBM. IBM hired the management consulting firm of Arthur D. Little to evaluate the opportunity, but they concluded that the total market for copy machines was only about 5,000 units. IBM passed, leaving Haloid to go forward on its own.

Beyond the impressive technology leap that made plain-paper copying possible, Wilson also engineered an innovative business model designed to alleviate the potential purchasing hurdles at large companies while also erecting barriers of entry for any future competitors. Instead of selling this new piece of office equipment, Haloid decided to lease its machines, making the upfront cost manageable and requiring fewer senior management approvals. The company earned its money on a "per copy" basis, getting paid every time users made a copy. To support this approach it built a national service and sales force to assist customers maximize the use of their new productivity tool, while also ensuring that Haloid sold its own specially-designed high-margin paper and toner.

The copier was relatively easy to use, but demonstrating this most salient feature required that the sales force transport heavy machines to potential client sites. Haloid had great success using a relatively new technology, television, to deliver the message of how simple it was to make plain-paper copies. By 1965, Haloid, having renamed itself Xerox Corporation, had grown annual revenues to a staggering $500 million with a trajectory promising incredible expansion. With a strong patent position and monopoly-like profit margins, Xerox became a juggernaut, dominating the worldwide office copier industry. A $10,000 investment in the company's shares in 1960 was worth over $1 million twelve years later.

In addition to a copy machine, standard-issue office automation in the late 1960s included rotary telephones, adding machines, typewriters, a telex machine, and Dictaphones. As Xerox grew and became a more powerful presence in the office, it turned its attention to an equally exciting emerging opportunity: data processing. IBM's computer business was too big to swallow, so Xerox went hunting for one of the other smaller, but fast-growing computer companies of the day, including Burroughs, Honeywell, Sperry, and Control Data. Getting no takers, management became desperate. Eventually, they found a willing seller, Scientific Data Systems, headquartered in Southern California. It had sales of approximately $100 million and only $10 million in profits, but Xerox was coaxed to pay a whopping $920 million for the company. Worse, SDS's computers were not designed to serve the office automation market Xerox planned to focus on, but instead had found their niche in scientific computing. Not surprisingly, while Xerox was looking to enter the computer business, Eastman Kodak and IBM, as well as several Japanese and German companies were eying the office copier business and had recognized that some of Xerox's fundamental patents would begin to expire and create an opening.

Xerox management had a much grander vision for its future role in office automation and the healthy cash flow to support it. Following in the footsteps of Thomas Edison's famed research center in Menlo Park, New Jersey, and seeing itself on the same elite stage as IBM, General Electric, RCA, Siemens, and AT&T, Xerox decided to build its own research laboratories so that it could remain on the cutting edge, a move that was consistent with its heritage of invention and innovation. The Xerox goal was to develop the "office of the future," design the "architecture of information," and position the company for the coming "paperless society" by becoming a leader in digital technologies while continuing to advance the analog imaging technology it had pioneered. It was a bold mission.

In 1970 Xerox opened its Palo Alto Research Center (Xerox PARC) near Stanford University, far from its corporate headquarters in Rochester, New York, and recruited many of the country's top computer scientists. PARC had no master plan or development program outlined at the beginning; its only guideline was that the researchers pursue areas of interest directionally consistent with Xerox's long-term mission of managing information.

AHEAD OF ITS TIME

At a time when large companies housed their data-processing machines in air-conditioned rooms behind glass walls staffed by highly trained technicians, with data entered via punch cards and tape, and teletype machines provided data output, PARC researchers began their work on a project with a radical concept. The PARC computer scientists foresaw that continuous advancement in semiconductor technology and software programming would reduce the cost of computing, and they wanted to ride that trend. They imagined a very different computing architecture in which the processing power and intelligence did not reside in a large, expensive, centralized machine, but instead could be distributed more locally to sit on an individual's desktop. To provide for interactivity and to get away from the batch processing and slow response times of existing computers, PARC wanted speed and connectivity. Their vision was simple: one machine per individual connected to other machines with shared peripherals, including printers. The one major drawback at the time was that the computer memory necessary to support a single user cost nearly $10,000, though PARC researchers expected the cost of memory chips and other electronics to decline significantly over time (within ten years the same amount of memory would cost only $30).

In 1971, PARC's scientists began work on a laser printer and Smalltalk, the first object-oriented programming language. Within two years they could display on a cathode ray tube (CRT) an image of the *Sesame Street* character Cookie Monster and had developed the basis for the Ethernet, a coaxial cable that would link each machine for direct communications using a local area network (LAN). By 1974, the system displayed bit-map graphics that allowed for pop-up menus, overlapping screen windows, point-and-click editing using a mouse, and the first user-friendly word processing system. Most impressive was the graphical user interface (GUI) controlled by a mouse that permitted users to avoid typing in long streams of code and esoteric commands.

PARC called their computer "the Alto." The Alto was designed by leading computer scientists for use by leading computer scientists so that they could more quickly develop even more impressive computer technology. Originally, PARC planned to manufacture thirty Altos for its engineers in the computer science lab. However, everyone at PARC seemed to want one. Ultimately, they built approximately 1,500 units for internal use and donated a few units to several universities. It was a powerful machine given the technology of the day: 128 kilobytes of main memory and a hard disk with a removable 2.5 megabyte cartridge and a black-on-white CRT display in portrait orientation. In addition to the innovative hardware configuration, the Alto broke new ground with its "what-you-see-is-what-you-get" (WYSIWYG) system—a technology that allowed, for the first time ever, taking the images on the screen and printing them exactly the same on a computer printer—email, word processing, and paint system software. Each Alto cost about $16,000, whereas a minicomputer ran approximately $100,000, and IBM was selling its fully-configured mainframe systems for millions of dollars.

When the January 1975 issue of *Popular Electronics*, a magazine for hobbyists, featured the Altair 8800, a computer for an individual user,[5] it quickly captured the imagination of many early computer scientists and young electronics nerds, including Bill Gates and Steve Jobs. For most of the world this was the first time the power of the computer was available, albeit quite primitively, for personal use. Priced at $397, the Altair 8800 was advertised as the first home computer, but it was really a hobbyist kit that had no software, keyboard, or display. It sold thousands of units. However, long before the introduction of the Altair 8800, Xerox PARC had developed its far more powerful, fully functioning, innovative hardware and software design that supported individual use and shared communications.

TROUBLE IN PARADISE

With the plain-paper copy machine Xerox had found and created a market that did not exist. It had revolutionized the office and developed a truly innovative business model. That was the company's legacy. But, when faced with a similar opportunity to commercialize the first personal computer a dozen years later, it had totally lost its mojo. Xerox, a company born out of exceptional innovation, could not marshal the corporate will to bring the personal computer to market. While the scientists at PARC were inventing the future of office automation, Xerox executives in Rochester, New York, were overwhelmed trying to protect their livelihoods. They were hit on multiple fronts. The steady rise of Japanese low-cost manufacturing being seen in consumer electronics and automobiles also began showing up in plain-paper copying in the mid-1970s led by Savin/Ricoh. Aggressive competition from U.S. computer giant IBM and cross-town rival Kodak rattled the Xerox management which had grown accustomed to their near-monopoly position. Moreover, the acquisition of SDS which had been acquired to provide the foundation for Xerox's move into computers had been a total bust. The SDS operation ran up over $100 million of losses, unable to compete with Digital Equipment's newest minicomputer, before shutting down in 1975.

In addition to unprecedented competition from new entrants, Xerox management was distracted by its legal battles with the U.S. government. A Federal Trade Commission (FTC) antitrust case against the company culminated in a settlement in 1975 requiring the company to share some of its important intellectual property, modify its pricing, and permit customers the right to buy toner from other suppliers. The global economic recession and inflation brought on by the abrupt increase in oil prices brought additional headwinds to Xerox, as the company's share price fell nearly 75 percent in the late 1970s.

Even against this backdrop Xerox management thought about commercializing some of the technology that its scientists had developed at PARC, setting up a new division with this specific goal in 1976. The following year PARC scientists, at a two-day conference in Florida, got the opportunity to demonstrate their new technology to the company's top management from around the world, but the long-haired big brains from Palo Alto clashed with the clean-cut "suits" from the rest of the organization. Even if the Alto, the Ethernet, and the laser printer impressed these executives, the SDS disaster made it difficult for them to contemplate entering the computer business. Moreover, given their preoccupation with protecting the huge cash flow from the copying business, Xerox was incapable of marketing a computer for the masses. After many years of being housed in a growing bureaucracy, primarily as order takers for Xerox copy machines, the company leadership had lost the appetite and skill for creating the business model and allocating the resources to introduce a radically new technology to the market.

By April 1979, Xerox executives in Rochester recognized that they lacked the wherewithal to bring PARC technology to market, so they turned their attention toward the hottest company in Silicon Valley, Apple Computer, founded by Steve Jobs and Steve Wozniak in 1976, following the introduction of the Altair 8800. The Apple I was a printed circuit board, which was more powerful than the Altair 8800, but still required assembly and connections for input and output devices. However, a year later the company introduced the Apple II, and for the first time consumers had a complete, affordable, fully-functioning personal computer with keyboard, display, and available application software. Xerox executives met with Steve Jobs to discuss an investment in his company. Having heard that Xerox had developed some remarkable computer technology, he agreed to let them invest in his company only after securing the opportunity to tour PARC. In December 1979, Jobs and several Apple employees received a complete demonstration of the Alto and its power. Jobs was overwhelmed: "They showed me really three things, but I was so blinded by the first one I didn't even really see the other two. One of the things they showed me was object-oriented programming. They showed me that, but I didn't even see that. The other one they showed me was a networked computer system that had over one hundred Alto computers all networked using email etc. I didn't even see that. I was so blinded by the first thing they showed me, which was the graphical user interface. I thought it was the best thing I'd ever seen in my life."[6]

For an investment of $1 million Xerox bought 2 percent of Apple Computer, ultimately turning a substantial profit after the Apple IPO in December 1980. But, Steve Jobs proved the big winner. Having seen the future charted by PARC, he then nimbly guided his team at Apple in developing the MacIntosh computer mimicking the functionality and architecture of the Alto, and totally revolutionizing personal computing for the next several decades. Xerox sold only 30,000 Alto computers before calling it quits. Its sales force showed more interest selling a typewriter that had some word processing functionality.

To become a leader in personal computers Xerox would have had to totally revamp its selling strategies, manufacturing operations, distribution channels, and mindset. Its historical business model of leasing copy machines was a poor template for the personal computer business. Moreover, it would have had to partner with other companies to write the application software that drives personal computer sales, an area that Xerox had no significant experience with. Its only potential winning course of action to bring a commercial personal computer to market would have been to run a separate business that was distinct from the cash-cow copying business, almost like its own start-up with an independent management team incentivized separately. Of course, to succeed Xerox would have needed the kind of entrepreneurial leadership it had had in its formative days from Joe Wilson.

Xerox PARC was hardly a failure though. The laser printer and other technology that it developed became the primary engine for Xerox's copying and printing business over the next thirty years, reminding us that large companies can earn great benefits from investing in research for the long-term.

*   *   *

Most people struggle to envision a world that is much different from their daily existence. We should not expect the majority of big companies to act differently. For some, the "not-invented-here" syndrome and layered decision making place tall hurdles in the way. For others, their management incentive systems and shareholder-driven short-term biases reward near-term performance making it less attractive to take the risk of entering a new business or thinking about a new business model for an existing business. Sometimes incumbent management gets too caught up with the challenges du jour, as did the management of Xerox, to devote the resources necessary for gestating businesses that do not conform to their current view of the world, and while charismatic CEO's often paint impressive roadmaps of the future plans for their enterprises, their organizations are not gated to bear the big risks inherent in implementing a radically different approach to a market. Sizable corporations work best by taking baby steps, not bold leaps. These substantial businesses possess many significant advantages over early stage ventures for tackling new markets, developing novel products, and leading the charge on innovation especially since their organizations tend to have relevant experience, access to capital, big R&D budgets, distribution channels, customer relationships, market credibility, and experienced managerial talent. But, with rare exception, they lack the essential ingredient for transformative success: entrepreneurial leadership; nimble people comfortable working without a well-worn template, roadmap or safety net.

CHAPTER 9

THE EPITOME OF INNOVATION

Good artists borrow, great artists steal.
—Pablo Picasso

STEVE JOBS, A COLLEGE DROP-OUT, DELIVERED THE 2005 commencement address at Stanford University, saying: "You've got to find what you love. Your work is going to fill a large part of your life, and the only way to be truly satisfied is to do what you believe is great work. And the only way to do great work is to love what you do." Jobs's advice is hard to argue with, and is made even more powerful because its source was perhaps the most influential, innovative, and consistently creative businessperson of the last one hundred years.

When Jobs personally paid $10 million to buy Pixar from George Lucas's Lucasfilm, Ltd. in 1986, the venture was an unprofitable division weighing down Lucas's lucrative film-making operations. Jobs saw in Pixar a high-end computer workstation company that targeted proprietary software technology for scientific and graphics-intensive applications. Over the next ten years, during which he divested Pixar's hardware division, Jobs poured an increasing amount of his dwindling personal wealth into a dream to harness the world's ever-increasing computing power and sophisticated software algorithms to create the next generation of animated film. During this period, Pixar made substantial leaps in computer animation technology, generating small amounts of revenue creating advertising, primarily for television. In 1995, Pixar finally broke through with the release of *Toy Story,* a feature-length film created totally on the computer and a story line developed inside the company. *Toy Story*'s worldwide box office exceeding $360 million made it the highest grossing movie of the year, positioning Jobs and the Pixar team to assume the mantle once held by Walt Disney as developers of a powerful new, leading-edge technology entertainment medium. Subsequent feature film releases by Pixar proved Jobs's vision and rewarded his perseverance. In 2006, Walt Disney Company paid $7.4 billion to acquire control of the company's film library, merchandising opportunities, animation technology, and creative team. In the process, Steve Jobs became the Walt Disney Company's largest individual shareholder. It seems fitting that Steve Jobs and Walt Disney, two of the most innovative entrepreneurs over the past century would have this strong connection. Steve Jobs's entrepreneurial capability and unique skillset most resembles Disney's. His rare combination of vision, drive for excellence, attention to detail, preparedness to take risk, showmanship, application of new technologies to establish industry leadership and competitive edge, and strong brand-building know-how reflected Walt Disney at his best. One should not overstate the connection, but the similarities are more than coincidence.

Pixar was Steve Jobs's second early stage company development effort. He could afford to undertake this investment solely because of the success of his first venture. The exciting story of Apple Computer's birth by two youngsters has been well documented. The legend of the "Steves," Jobs and Wozniak, and their April Fool's Day, 1976, launch of the Apple I from Jobs's garage in Silicon Valley exemplifies the powerful notion of transformative product innovation. Introduced in 1977, the early Apple Computer models, most specifically the Steve Wozniak–designed Apple II with its 8-bit microprocessor, keyboard, disk drive, operating system, and color graphics was a marvel of hardware engineering tied to the first wave of useful software applications and affordable computer peripherals. Aided by venture capital from established West Coast firms and adult supervision from an experienced cadre of Silicon Valley executives, led by Mike Markkula a young, but recently retired Intel marketing manager, Apple Computer catalyzed the personal computer industry much as Ken Olsen's Digital Equipment Corporation had done twenty years earlier with minicomputers. Although initial applications of personal computer technology were limited, the introduction of VisiCalc, the first computer spreadsheet, marketed by VisiCorp in 1979, made personal computers useful for business work and propelled the demand for the new machines.

Apple was the primary beneficiary of this increased demand because of its sleek design and relatively superior compute power. However, when IBM introduced its first PC in 1981 with the full faith and backing of "Big Blue," Apple woke up one day to find that it had a new formidable competitor, one that was not used to taking any prisoners in its quest for dominant worldwide market share.

The world's largest computer systems company, with many thousands of white-shirted, highly trained professional salespeople, legitimized the personal computer in the business community; no longer were PCs solely a toy for hobbyists and early adopters. IBM had licensed the operating system for its PC from a young Seattle-based company, Microsoft, which had sold an identical system to other new personal computer manufacturers. Quickly, IBM and its clones captured an increasingly large share of the market, as third-party application software developers began focusing their efforts on the biggest portion of the pie. While elegant hardware design and brand name meant something to early buyers of personal computers, their purchase decisions were based primarily on getting low-cost machines that ran the software applications they needed to do their work or to have fun. IBM and Microsoft executed a strategy that was superior to Apple's. To regain the upper hand, Steve Jobs set about to create the second great commercial product innovation in personal computing.

TRANSITORY EXCELLENCE

In 1984 Apple introduced the Macintosh, the first affordable personal computer with a graphical user interface, which forever changed the way humans interacted with computers. While much of the Macintosh's architecture and functionality was lifted from the technology that had been developed at Xerox PARC in the 1970s, Jobs and his team at Apple proved once again that the spoils often go to those who commercialize technology, not those who invent it. Although the Macintosh was not a financial success until Apple created the market for desktop publishing, it served as the primary cornerstone for the company's survival when the IBM PC, and its clones, captured an overwhelming share of the personal computer market.

When Steve Jobs was fired from Apple in 1985 for not playing well in the sandbox with others at Apple, especially its CEO John Scully, he created NeXT Computer to go after a much higher-end segment of the computer market, bringing with him his commanding managerial strengths: attention to detail, a relentless desire to make great products, a strong aesthetic around industrial design, determination and a drive to succeed, demanding expectations for all those who worked with and for him, and charismatic leadership. Despite significant capital infusions from H. Ross Perot and Canon, NeXT was not a success in a traditional business sense, but it did create a leading-edge operating system that formed the basis for Jobs's reentry into Apple in 1997, when he sold his new company to his old one.

Apple was a money-losing mess hard-wired into a downward spiral when Jobs returned to the helm. It had taken Microsoft many years to create a competitive operating system to compete with the Macintosh, but with the introduction of Windows 95, it got the upper hand. Apple's board was desperate to get its founding light back because the company had lost its way from a product, profit, and cultural perspective. Through a combination of aggressive cost-cutting, strategic reorientation, a streamlined product mix, new computer product introductions, the raising of capital, and external relationship building, Jobs turned Apple around within a few years, positioning it for its next great leap forward. As before, Jobs's innate sense of design would play an important role in creating high functionality in a personal computer package that screamed "cool." In a product category known for drab and boxy, Apple's emphasis on creative design rivaled that of Knoll's office furniture, Bang & Olafson's entertainment equipment, Ducati's motorcycles, and Nike's footwear.

One of the many things that Steve Jobs learned during his tenure as head of a computer company is the power of owning a platform product or service. Microsoft's nearly ubiquitous Windows operating system had turned thousands of its employees into millionaires by creating its superior market position, while Apple had consistently struggled against its stronger competitor. Always a believer in maintaining strict control of the customers' entire product experience, Jobs insisted that Apple implement a strategy of closely integrated product development and design. Apple therefore bundled its hardware and software (and many of the peripherals). However, if the only thing a company has is great product, especially in the fast-paced technology sector, it remains vulnerable to competitors that continually try to leap-frog each other. IBM and others had proved that product is only part of what customers consider in making their personal computer buying decision. They also paid attention to product support, useful software availability, network integration, and low cost. Given the rapidity of technological change in this sector, which drives improved functionality at reduced cost, participants in the computer industry regularly confront eroding profit margins.

To take his company to new heights, Jobs meticulously transformed Apple, beginning in 2001, from a personal computer company into the world's leading consumer electronics company, initially emulating and then surpassing Sony, a company Jobs had admired during his early years. As always, Jobs started by designing great product, but this time the business models were different, radically different. Instead of placing Apple on the typical technology company treadmill of ever-improving compute power and software friendliness, Jobs morphed the strategy to take advantage of the superior profit-making potential of developing an integrated system that was more akin to the holistic business models implemented by Southwest Airlines and IKEA. Leveraging off of the technology developments of other companies, Apple pulled together a brilliant set of entrees that continue to reshape the global consumer entertainment and information experience while simultaneously attacking the turf of the more mature consumer electronics, Internet-enabled, increasingly wireless, players.

YOU SAY YOU WANT A REVOLUTION

In 2001 Apple started to remake itself, introducing the now ubiquitous iPod and revolutionizing the music publishing industry. Its original products were hard-drive-based music players featuring sleek design, an intuitive user interface, distinctive white ear buds, capacity to hold over 1,000 songs, and retailing for nearly $400. Other companies had pioneered MP3 music players, but Apple took the technology and product concept to a new dimension. Two years later Apple furthered its market position by launching the iTunes Music Store, following Steve Jobs's intensive and persistent eighteen-month negotiation with music industry executives for digital music rights, which resulted in a legal revenue-sharing model that allowed users to download music at a cost of $0.99 per song. The music industry business model that had been destined for long-term decline because of Napster had a new lease on life. Jobs had implemented a creative arrangement with the music publishing industry, a group of companies most noted for never agreeing about anything. The primary technology behind Apple's iTunes was a proprietary system of digital-rights management that encrypted songs so that they could work only with iPods, preventing peer-to-peer file sharing. A standard MP3 file did not play on iPods; it required a special conversion to Apple's compression format. Moreover, iTunes provided a user-friendly interface, and a database library for storing and sorting music, and creating desired playlists. The combination of great hardware (iPod) with great software (iTunes) and ease of use in downloading songs legally and relatively inexpensively made Apple a huge winner. Initially, iTunes and the Music Store were accessible only through Apple computers, but in 2003, in a seemingly uncharacteristic but deft strategic move, Apple opened the system to attract the far larger market of Windows 2000–based computers. In an instant the market for iTunes and iPods exploded, giving Apple a highly profitable business platform that it could control. By 2006 iTunes customers had already downloaded 1 billion songs from an ever-broadening music catalog, and by early 2010 the tally reached 10 billion. Not shy about expansion, Apple began to use the iTunes Music Store as the foundation for disseminating other digital entertainment content, including TV shows, videos, movies, and radio broadcasts. Before long, iPod became the de facto standard for MP3 players, and the direct tie into iTunes and the Music Store made the switching cost for its customers very high. They were locked in. Apple had created a complete product and service offering with very high entry barriers for competitors and very high exit barriers for customers, thereby positioning the company for strong profitability. Jobs had turned the traditional razor-razor blade business model on its head. Instead of selling the razor at a low price to attract repeat customers for the high-margin proprietary razor blade, Apple gave away the software (iTunes) to attract people to pay up for high-margin iPods, and began its transition from a computer company to a consumer electronics company. This led to its subsequent renaming as "Apple, Inc.," dropping "Computer."

This same attention to design and detail was evident in Apple's successful entry into retailing, opening its new Apple Stores. The stores maintained a minimalist feel but captured the target market in a way that no other computer retailer or consumer electronics chain had ever done. Other personal computer retailers, such as Gateway, had rolled out retail stores, but they did not succeed, eventually closing after large quantities of red ink had been spilled, and many pundits predicted the same outcome for Apple. Such innovations as the Genius Bar, the stores' on-site help desk, brought customers in and also gave them the opportunity to play with new products and hang out with fellow Apple devotees. As with most things Apple, Jobs was the prime creator of the retailing concept and its implementation, and he ensured that every aspect of the Apple Store met his high standards of quality and style. For the retail division Jobs also tapped outside talent, specifically Ron Johnson, who left Target in 2000 to lead the Apple Store effort.[1] Today there are well over three hundred Apple Stores throughout the world and the number is growing, furthering the image of the company and its products. As long as the company churns out winning new products, the Stores should continue to generate huge profits while maintaining the allure of the Apple brand.

Apple's subsequent breakthrough products, the iPhone in 2007 and the iPad in 2010, provided similar integrated and protected product and market positioning. Once again, elegant design and great functionality underpinned the foundation of a highly successful product line, totally in keeping with the company's design legacy and Apple's newfound emphasis on owning the platform. Apple did not pioneer the smart-phone or the tablet computer, but it took those inventions to entirely new levels from a product and business-model perspective. The intro-duction of the App Store, a separate catalog of third-party-developed applications, including games, business tools, travel websites, and so on, allowed customers to easily download software from newly formed inde-pendent start-up companies that provided enhanced features, stickiness, and impressive profits for Apple. The iPhone and the iPad are outstand-ing products in their own right and have a clear competitive edge over existing "smart" mobile devices. However, the App Store provides the glue for iPhones and iPads just as iTunes has for the iPod. Once custom-ers pay for and load many different apps onto their iPhones and iPads, the exit barriers to switch platforms grows too high and provides Apple with a huge competitive advantage. Customers have downloaded over 15 billion apps thus far. These platforms, and the sexy execution, have given the company a commanding lead over the competition. Not only had Apple once again shown great product innovation, but it also has a business-model innovation that protects them for the long term, pro-ducing astounding levels of quarterly cash flows.

Proprietary products and systems that are cool to own and offer high functionality provided a fabulous recipe for success. Steve Jobs, for many years a victim of Microsoft's near-monopoly control of the operating system, learned his lessons extremely well and vaulted his company, now a consumer electronics giant, into the pole position. Not surprisingly, as the Apple brand strengthened, the strong demand for consumer products began to drag along increasing sales of its personal computers and laptops.

Today, despite Apple's large size, innovation remains firmly embedded in its DNA. What sets Apple apart from many other large companies is that its entrepreneurial genesis and founder-led passion and risk-taking have created a culture that will risk failure and that incentivizes creativity. Apple has demonstrated that companies don't have to invent each new product offering from scratch but can tailor existing leading-edge products and commercialize them successfully. From its origins in the mid-1970s Apple has taken advantage of new technology, the pioneering products of others, and its own sense of what customers want to consistently introduce winners. Of course, Apple has had many new product failures,[2] but that has been a small price to pay given the huge success of its new, high-quality products and business models.

More importantly, Apple recognizes that its products are a means to an end, not an end in themselves; its real long-term profit drivers are the products that form parts of systems or platforms in a broader integrated customer offering. This position is much more defensible than the one Apple had when it was focused solely on the personal computer. As computer and communications technologies continue to improve and converge, they propel Apple's confrontation with established companies, such as Google, Amazon.com, Research-In-Motion, Microsoft, Nokia, and Samsung. Moreover, start-up companies abound, aided by venture capital. Apple has a full suite of competitors focused on specific product lines and market segments, which are all working to grab some of its market share.

Simultaneously fighting competitive wars on many fronts has, historically, brought companies to their knees and diluted their resources when they lacked the scale and managerial intensity to successfully defend their turf. In Xerox's heyday in the 1960s, it was one of the great companies behind the copier technology that it had initiated and dominated. But, Xerox found it hard to stay on top when their technology edge ebbed and the demands of directing a large global business destroyed the entrepreneurial genes of the company. Apple may face the same challenge in the future in managing its own worldwide organization and broadening product lines, especially since its business units today offer personal computers, music players, smart phones, and form factors in between. Time will tell if Apple can manage its way through this convergence of global competitors, technology advancements, and market forces. Fortunately, it has several key ingredients for success already in place—considerable momentum and a very healthy balance sheet.

ATOP THE LEADER BOARD

It is only the rarest entrepreneur who starts a company, oversees its climb to scale, and then continues to dominate its strategy and execution for many years thereafter. Bill Gates did it. Herb Kelleher at Southwest Airlines did it. Fred Smith at FedEx and Jeff Bezos at Amazon.com still do it. Michael Dell at Dell Computer and Howard Schultz at Starbucks reclaimed their CEO positions, both returning to right the ship after their companies had seemingly lost their magic. The skills and temperament to start a business are not the same as those required to build a business. Normally, the founders pass the baton to more seasoned executives, sometimes acquiescing and sometimes needing a less than gentle shove. From the perspective of innovation, entrepreneurial companies whose founders are still pushing their companies forward often have a distinct advantage over those that have ceded managerial leadership to executives whose skills are more attuned to supervising large enterprises, managing staff, and massaging Wall Street investors. Conversely, Henry Ford held on too long to the company he started, remaining wedded to his Model T philosophy as others, including Alfred Sloan at General Motors, ran past him with more modern strategies that were better attuned to contemporary times. But, it is hard to beat the passion, intensity, protectiveness, and affection the founder of a business provides. These entrepreneurs understand the importance of taking risks and pushing ahead when others fear making mistakes. They understood, at a very deep level, the unparalleled feeling of accomplishment from betting everything on a dream and winning.

Over the course of his career Jobs launched the personal computer industry and then redefined it eight years later, ushered in new levels of motion picture animation, revolutionized the music publishing industry, and then created distinctive smartphone and tablet product segments with innovative and lucrative business models. He has been the maestro driving his organization to excellence, leading from the front, taking charge, demanding performance, and willing to be wrong. If there was a "Hall of Fame" for business innovation there is little doubt that Steve Jobs would lead the first class of inductees.

The elephant in the room regarding Apple's future remains the long-term fate of the company now that its icon has passed away. How does Apple replace Steve Jobs? How does Apple maintain its innovation edge and culture to "think different"? How does Apple continue to churn out products that are "insanely great" and supportive of business models that generate abnormally high levels of profitability?

A departed founder/entrepreneur, especially one who has led the creative efforts and set the culture of a company, often leaves a large hole in an organization. Walt Disney is long gone but it took his company many years to find its footing in his absence. Bill Gates now oversees his family foundation full-time, and many would say that Microsoft lost its competitive edge with his departure. But some companies successfully transition leadership after their founders depart. Yet, Apple seems different, due perhaps in part to its twelve years of wandering in the desert without Steve Jobs in the 1990s, and because Jobs had attained cult-leader status for the many millions of Apple product followers who adore everything that he stood for. The near-term future for the company seems secure with strong market positions in its selected niches, and a product pipeline that will continue to meet needs consumers don't yet know they have. After that, Apple will stand on its own, beyond the founder's direct influence, and operate in the shadow of entrepreneurial genius.

CHAPTER 10

VENTURESOME CAPITAL

The entrepreneur and the financier are the interdependent wheels turning innovation forward.

—Joseph Schumpeter

MOST ENTREPRENEURS STRUGGLE TO ACCESS THE CAPITAL NEEDED TO start and grow a business for one simple reason: the vast majority of new businesses fail, delivering little or no return to those who put up the money. Ideas that appeared so exciting on paper and that are brought to life by entrepreneurs who are seemingly destined for success end up in disappointment, with misery and financial loss for those who took the upfront risk. However, nearly all new businesses aspiring to reach meaningful scale require some sort of outside funding to get established and even more money to finance a rapid growth trajectory. The funds to start and grow a business often come from personal savings, friends, family, and support from customers and suppliers. Entrepreneurs usually find that these sources of funds have a low effective cost of capital in terms of dilution, though there is clearly some added pain if your father-in-law loses money if your new venture fails.

Fortunately, a business model that is not capital intensive or that generates an early positive cash flow through high profit margins substantially reduces the magnitude of required outside financing, leaving more ownership for the founders and management teams. Bill Gates and his co-founders never required third-party financing to launch Microsoft in 1978 because personal computer software development had relatively low upfront costs, especially considering that the programmers lived in cheap motels and subsisted on cold pizza and Coke. In 1981, Microsoft decided to tap into the advice of one Silicon Valley venture capitalist, and although the company did not need the money, it accepted a $1 million investment in exchange for a 5 percent ownership stake. Microsoft's management retained the rest of the ownership, which explains one reason why Mr. Gates consistently holds a prominent position on the *Forbes 400*.

Similarly, Bill Hewlett and David Packard, the founders of the company that bears their names, bootstrapped the company's beginnings from the famed garage in Palo Alto, California, in 1938. Their early products, including a signaling device for the local bowling alley foul line, a controller for the Lick Observatory telescope, and a low-cost audio oscillator that was used in Disney's famed *Fantasia,* were custom designed and paid for promptly by the customer. And due to their proprietary nature and high intellectual content, they generated substantial profit margins, which the founders promptly reinvested to feed their company's growth. Hewlett and Packard never raised any outside capital until the company's successful IPO in 1957. Both retired from the company as billionaires.

Conversely, as we have seen, in the 1970s Federal Express required substantial outside capital to move from Fred Smith's initial concept to a self-sustaining enterprise. Federal Express tapped numerous resources including Smith's personal funds, family funds, venture capital, bank loans, and corporate loans before reaching the scale and profitability that would support its IPO. Smith had little choice; the Federal Express business plan necessitated buying lots of expensive equipment and undergoing years of losses until the company gained a sufficient volume of packages to create positive cash flow. Fred Smith owned only 12 percent of Federal Express when it went public.

Today, many new ventures targeting alternative energy—*cleantech*—face this conundrum: the need to raise large amounts of upfront capital and having large, fixed-cost business models to help try to wean the world off its dependency on coal and oil. New businesses seeking to make oil from biofuels or to turn coal into natural gas have to ramp up their facilities and technology in stages, from lab bench to pilot scale to full production. Each stage of growth must demonstrate a pathway to attractive economics to support the financing plan for the next iteration of the technology at a larger manufacturing plant. Similarly, facilities to mass produce solar cells and package them into modules also require tens of millions if not hundreds of millions of dollars of upfront capital investment. Without this outlay for leading-edge factories, the companies lack the manufacturing capability and the opportunity to slide down the experience curve. While high capital needs create an entry barrier for future competition, they also create a huge hurdle for the young enterprise.

New biotechnology companies usually have the same hefty capital requirement as cleantech businesses because the product-development cycle and regulatory-approval processes often span ten years, and success is hardly a certain outcome. In the process these companies consume huge amounts of risk capital—mostly equity—to cover the upfront expenditures.

Twenty-first-century innovation can be expensive and risky. This combination repels most investors. Unless potential investors see the prospect of very large returns, they won't line up to risk their capital, especially a lot of capital. The challenge for entrepreneurs who need these funds to build their businesses, and the challenge for national economies that need the entrepreneurs and their ideas to fuel growth and employment is in creating the right combination of incentives and protections to encourage investors to take the necessary risks. Fortunately, there is a class of investors and investment professionals, increasingly located throughout the world, who relish the risk-reward of nurturing new entrepreneurial enterprises.

RISKY BUSINESS

An old Yiddish proverb tells us: "With money in your pocket, you are wise and you are handsome—and you sing well too." Legendary investor Warren Buffett, the Oracle of Omaha, once remarked that "a fool and his money are soon invited everywhere." It is an uncommon luxury to have considerable money to invest, but if you do, then your popularity and perceived intellect increase proportionately. Although the attention can make you feel powerful, omniscient, and important, investing money, especially other people's money, also comes with responsibility, decision-making, risk-taking, and an omnipresent scorecard. Most investment professionals are capable of telling great stories, displaying charismatic charm, offering masterful salesmanship, while spinning creative and differentiated investment strategies, rarely do they consistently outperform average public equity market performance levels. It is a rare breed of investor that year-in, year-out demonstrates results that outshine those of peers. Why? Despite the findings of their numerous academic studies and the protestations of many hedge fund managers, investing is not a science but an art form. Even with access to modern technology, ultrafast computers, Ph.D.–authored proprietary algorithms, artificial-intelligence-based expert systems, and bearing the scars from decades of past experience, consistently generating rates of return in excess of standard benchmarks over long periods of time is very hard to do.

The work of venture capitalists, angel investors, and others who dare to put up risk capital to help launch and grow new businesses is central to an entrepreneurial economy. There is little doubt that venture capital, as practiced in the United States, has been a huge driver of the nation's economic growth and technological leadership for the past forty years. An estimated 11 percent of all those employed in the U.S. private sector today work for companies who garnered venture capital support in their early years. These companies now account for over 20 percent of the GDP of the United States and include many of the fastest growing corporations in the nation. Moreover, many studies have highlighted that employment growth over the past thirty years in the United States has come predominantly from entrepreneurial businesses, suggesting an important connection between risk capital availability and fundamental economic development.

This extraordinarily impressive list of companies includes Adobe, Amazon.com, AmGen, AOL, Apple, Baidu, BEA Systems, Biogen, Celgene, Cisco, Compaq, eBay, Facebook, Fedex, Genentech, Gilead, Google, Intuit, Microsoft, Home Depot, Intel, JetBlue, Juniper Networks, Kosmos Energy, LSI Logic, Medtronic, Netscape, Nvidia, PayPal, Skype, Spinnaker Exploration, Staples, Starbucks, Stryker, Sun Microsystems, Teradyne, Tesla Motors, 3Com, Twitter, U.S. Healthcare, and Yahoo! as just a few of many thousands of examples. Each one attracted the financial resources and managerial expertise of the U.S. venture capital community, and have enjoyed outstanding commercial success and generated positive investment returns for their shareholders while also becoming huge winners for their entrepreneurial founders, employees, customers, investors, and supporters.

Sadly, the size of the list of failed venture capital-backed companies completely dwarfs the list of winners. These failed companies were started with the best of intentions by thoughtful, hard-working, well-meaning, risk-taking people, but for numerous reasons never got scale. And some burned through tens of millions of dollars of equity capital before they were put to sleep. Maybe their failure reflected an inadequate product idea, or leadership that lacked the incentive or ability to hustle, or a changing market that left them behind, or an entrenched competitor that proved to be more nimble than expected. The reasons behind entrepreneurial failure are nearly infinite, further supporting the notion that entrepreneurial success requires excellence across all the major business disciplines. Losing money in search of high potential reward is endemic to the investment business, and why "many a pessimist got that way by financing an optimist."

Business success stems from the thousands of decisions that entrepreneurs make in the formative stages of an enterprise, when resources are tight, when the immediate world is telling them that their idea won't work, when the competition seems all-powerful, when capital is hard to find, when naysayers far outnumber supporters, and when recruiting quality people to the cause is most important. Of these thousands of decisions, some are small, others big, some brilliant, and others fatal. Access to capital and a support network for entrepreneurial CEO's provided by venture capitalists can mean the difference between success and failure. Venture capitalists earn their keep by working closely with management teams, not as operators, but as advisors and board members, with the singular objective of increasing shareholder value. The venture capitalist plays a value-added role, letting management fight the daily battles of the business, keeping a bit above the fray to maintain perspective and long-term orientation, acting as sounding boards, taking emotion out of the decision-making process, and pushing the management team's analytical rigor. The management teams and the venture capitalists that invest behind them have aligned economic interests in the quest for the best decision and direction, minimizing the potential for conflict.

Sometimes, when entrepreneurs are trying to raise outside financing, they focus too much on getting a high valuation and protecting their ownership percentage, forgetting that the primary goal is building a successful business, especially one that can get to scale. The objective of management should be accessing sufficient capital and experienced counsel to help the venture succeed. Most young businesses fail due to undercapitalization, and most entrepreneurs would benefit substantially from the objective advice of those who have walked the company-building path before, suggesting that there is a prominent and important role for experienced venture capitalists.

Of course, accessing venture capital does not guarantee success and sometimes comes with other constraints, but selecting good partners who bring funding, experience, outside networks, and credibility more likely will increase, not hinder, the probability of success. Besides, they tend to work with their new ventures without asking for salaries, consulting fees or bonuses, only piggybacking on the potential appreciation of the underlying shares that they buy.

FINANCING INNOVATION

Venture capitalists love to talk about their industry drawing its roots and inspirations from Queen Isabella and King Ferdinand of Spain, who over five hundred years ago sponsored the original voyage of Christopher Columbus to find the westward route to the West Indies. But institutionalized venture capital, itself a significant innovation in finance and a foundation for entrepreneurial activity, formally began in the United States in the 1940s. Other than the funds that were sometimes available from wealthy families like the Rockefellers and Vanderbilts, whose notable venture capital investments included Eastern Airways and Pan American Airways, risk capital was a rarity.

Commercial banks have never been anxious or staffed to provide funding for companies with very limited assets, without positive cash flow, and no track record of profitability. The traditional bank lending model risk-return trade-off is not compatible with funding early stage ventures. As Mark Twain remarked: "A banker is a fellow who lends you his umbrella when the sun is shining and wants it back the minute it begins to rain."[1] Banks do not expect to lose money on most of their loans. Conversely, venture capitalists understand that many of their investments won't succeed, but they need some to succeed exceptionally well to more than cover the cost of those investments that do not work out.

In 1946, J.H. "Jock" Whitney, who had inherited about $200 million from his father in the 1930s, allocated about $10 million of his personal wealth to create funding to nurture new enterprises. He started an investment fund in New York that would treat venture capital as a business staffed by full-time professionals involved in analyzing investment opportunities, making investments, and then working with the management teams they supported. His insight was that while early stage businesses need capital, they also need managerial guidance. Whitney wanted his firm to provide both, believing that the investment returns would be better if his team worked alongside the entrepreneurs to assist their strategy development and implementation. He had some success, most notably providing financing after World War II for the National Research Corporation which had developed a process for concentrating orange juice. National Research Corporation eventually changed its name to Minute Maid, and venture capital was on the board.

At the same time as Jock Whitney was creating an active approach to funding and fostering new businesses, a consortium of business and educational leaders in Boston raised outside funding to try to help the suffering New England economy. With the traditional local manufacturing businesses of shoe-making and textiles declining, these thoughtful gentlemen concluded that it might be profitable to provide small amounts of financing for new businesses that took advantage of the research coming out of the local universities and for the technology companies that had worked with the U.S. government in the war effort. Led by French-born Harvard Business School professor Georges Doriot, a new company was set up to raise third-party funding from several universities and insurance companies. Doriot also thought that it would be valuable to train specialists in venture capital, and with the $3.5 million in equity he raised he hired a small staff and went out to find, evaluate, and support investment opportunities for his new firm, American Research & Development—AR&D.

Whereas J.H. Whitney's investment approach was an extension of the Rockefeller and Vanderbilt families' investment office model, AR&D was the first independent firm formed solely to provide risk capital by raising its funds from outside investors and professionalizing the practice of making investments in and then supporting entrepreneurial companies with strategic advice and guidance. Their track record was uneven. Early successes, such as High Voltage Engineering Corp.—a manufacturer of particle accelerators used initially for medical applications and Zapata Oil, led by George H.W. Bush, balanced a fair number of failures. Fortunately for AR&D, and ultimately for the U.S. venture capital industry, in 1957 Doriot's team discovered a new opportunity inside M.I.T.'s Lincoln Laboratories, where Ken Olsen was developing a powerful new data-processing machine that was smaller than the big mainframes produced by IBM and was architected for department-level computing, often of a scientific nature. Olsen's machine used transistors instead of vacuum tubes and interactive data entry instead of punch card batch-processing methods. Olsen agreed to sell Doriot approximately 70 percent of his new company, Digital

Equipment Corporation (DEC), in exchange for $70,000 of equity funding—a considerable amount of money at the time. DEC launched the minicomputer industry and went on to become a behemoth, growing very quickly and profitably, and spawning numerous other computer companies in the Boston area. When AR&D sold its stake in DEC in 1971 its $70,000 investment was worth approximately $350 million. Both the entrepreneurial and investment communities really began taking notice of venture capital.

Jock Whitney and Georges Doriot never expected that their innovation—making venture capital a systematic professional service—would create a new industry, a new investment asset class, and most importantly, erect a fundamental pillar for U.S. economic growth and technological commercialization. But it did.

VALUE-ADDED INVESTORS

At its heart venture capital is an investment business that involves soliciting funds from wealthy families and institutions, and then, hopefully, over time, returning multiples of the initial capital to those who took the upfront risk. Facilitating rates of return in excess of those of the public equity markets required venture capital professionals to contribute more than money, they needed to assist the entrepreneurial management teams in making key decisions, formulating strategic direction, recruiting senior management talent and board members, designing incentive compensation systems, structuring financing plans, including IPOs, and supporting the broader tasks of building the business by helping with sales, vendor relationships, and joint ventures. As more and more young companies aspired to participate in international markets, the more experienced venture capital organizations built skills sets and relationships to facilitate such growth.

Successful venture capitalists learned that it was not their job to directly manage the companies they invested in, but to ensure that they were well-managed. Moreover, because they were investors in the business aligned with management and other shareholder interests, the venture capitalists could bring significant experience in the art of growing a business having participated in this effort many times in the past and amassing the scars of previous lessons learned. As the CEO's confidant the venture capitalist could provide a distinct perspective and wisdom to the often "its lonely at the top" leader, and also play the role of cheerleader when inevitable bumps in the road emerged. Some venture capital firms developed high-quality reputations and impressive track records. Their portfolio of companies benefited from a halo effect, which improved their credibility and enhanced the potential of the business, easing the recruitment process for new employees supporting customer and vendor relationships, and boosting the odds that the early stage company would gain firm footing on the road to prosperity.

Not lost on the venture capitalist was the fundamental understanding that in exchange for accepting the illiquidity that comes from buying shares in private enterprises, they needed to have the ability to exert some influence or control. While the shareholders of public companies always have the ability to cash out of their investments very quickly if they lose confidence in a company's direction or leadership, the venture capitalists' investment in a private company with no active trading market meant that they were stuck in a challenging investment if they did not like the progress of the company. Once the money went in, it was hard to get it out, especially on a timely basis and especially without taking a significant haircut on its value. As active investors and highly interested parties, venture capitalists often initiate changes in the senior management of the companies that they invest in if performance levels do not meet expectations. Some entrepreneurs recognize that those who prove invaluable in launching a business frequently are not the same people that excel at growing or managing a business. Ultimately, the venture capitalists remain loyal to the objectives of the shareholders of the company, not the founders or individual managers. As active investors with money at risk and a focus on the long-term growth of their portfolio companies, venture capitalists play an important value-added role supporting and nurturing the entrepreneurial economy.

Equally important, venture capitalists in the United States have become economic gatekeepers, rationing risk capital throughout the entrepreneurial community. Sitting at the crossroads of capital and entrepreneurialism, they are well-positioned to sift through the numerous investment opportunities and decide which companies deserve access to the limited amounts of available equity. Today, leading venture capital firms each receive thousands of new investment opportunities every year. They choose to fund only a handful that appear to have the proper mix of management talent, growth potential, an attractive business model, and a defensible competitive position. Even with a thorough filtering process they face long odds of success mostly because it is not a business of black and white analysis or binary outcomes, but rather one of judgment, creativity, and a willingness to venture into the unknown and unknowable.

As new companies increasingly accessed venture capital in the 1980s to finance their lift-off and growth phases, an entire ecosystem grew up to support the creation of entrepreneurial enterprises, including law firms, contract service providers, entrepreneurial support groups, executive-recruiting and public-relations professionals, and a cadre of investment banking firms anxious to bring the most successful of these companies to the public equity markets, where they could access the less expensive equity needed to reach the next level of performance. The IPO reinforced the venture capital business model, allowing investors and the management teams that they financed to reap substantial benefits, providing a pathway to liquidity that would complete the life cycle of investment and harvest. Moreover, with spreading publicity and attention from the mass media around the highest flyers, probably beginning with Genentech's IPO in 1980, and a succession of personal computer-related companies soon thereafter, successful entrepreneurs became the role models and poster children for other aspiring entrepreneurs. More visible success meant more entrepreneurial activity, which in turn drove more money into venture capital funds, each requiring more support services and reinforcing a wonderful positive spiral. It became relatively easy to launch new businesses and spur economic growth. With a well-established template and resource pool available, meeting the entrepreneurial urges of this community became much easier and quicker. Everybody won.

The advent of a user-friendly Internet, initially powered by Netscape's browser in the mid-1990s, allowed the U.S. venture capital industry to emerge from the shadows. No longer a cottage industry, it took center stage, becoming the subject of mainstream business magazine cover stories, with the best and brightest of its practitioners achieving rock star status. As a steadily growing asset class in many institutional investor portfolios from the mid-1970s, U.S. venture capital funds were investing about $10 billion annually by the mid-1990s. However, the compressed cycle of initial investment-to-liquidity in Internet-land propelled the annual investment run-rate over $100 billion by 1999. But, as with most things in life, including money, too much of a good thing can be hazardous to your health. Venture capital and the new businesses it funded were no different. Average investment rates of return for the venture capital industry, which had skyrocketed to well over 100 percent in 1999, went negative in 2001 as the flood of money that had financed many new businesses that lacked a good reason to exist or a business model that could generate positive cash flow rapidly receded. When the Internet bubble deflated, this cycle of venture capital's heyday ended with a thud. For those few who had liquefied their investments in time, it was a doubly enjoyable journey. But, most venture capital firms held on too long, either lacking the liquidity to cash out or believing their own hype. These firms got little out of the bubble for themselves or for those that provided the capital.

Far from perfect, the venture capital industry in the United States has experienced its share of disappointment and self-inflicted pain. Overzealousness and occasional greed diverted some firms from practicing their profession with skill and judgment. For some entrepreneurs, venture capital came to mean "vulture capital." They felt taken advantage of when the supply-demand curve tipped in favor of those with money who exercised their version of the Golden Rule: "he who hath the gold makes the rules". During the first ten years of the new millennium, relatively poor average rates of return compared to standard publicly-traded equity metrics caused the venture capital industry to fall out of favor with institutional investors. A dearth of IPOs and other high-flying investment themes demoted venture capitalists from cover story icons in the business press to yesterday's news. Nonetheless, the ecosystem survives, awaiting the next wave of opportunity, technology, or excessive public equity market behavior. History suggests that the industry rates of return are cyclical and that another catalyst will emerge to drive equity prices higher and bring the venture capital industry back into the limelight, where it remains well-positioned to support entrepreneurs and sponsor new innovations.

CHAPTER 11

NOBLE ENDEAVORS

Goodness is the only investment that never fails.
—Henry David Thoreau

IN TODAY'S CHAOTIC TIMES, MANY NEW ENTREPRENEURS SEEK TO make
a difference without focusing on making a profit. Entrepreneurship is
not always about generating shareholder wealth. Sometimes that happens, but entrepreneurship is mostly about developing and building sustainable new enterprises around creative ideas and innovative business
models. And if the principles apply to the for-profit sector why not apply
them to the not-for-profit sector? The need is great; the opportunities are
large; and the returns, potentially very impactful. "Social entrepreneurship," the application of entrepreneurial practices in the not-for-profit
sector, continues to grow rapidly in the United States and around the
world because it works. The best way to help people rise above the poverty line, improve their health care, or upgrade their educational experience is not solely to give money to charitable institutions, but instead
to provide the time and expertise so that they can help themselves. For
example, we see this with organizations such as the Acumen Fund, a
venture capital fund that supports entrepreneurs in the developing world
by providing funding and managerial expertise to early stage companies
in the housing, health care, water, agriculture, and energy industries,
and often taking an ownership stake in the fledgling companies. As
with any venture capital fund, Acumen wants to generate acceptable
rates of return, but it measures that return not only on a dollar basis, but
also on a social impact basis. There are thousands of nongovernmental
organizations around the world led by entrepreneurial people who are
deploying new ways to improve the standard of living and quality of

life. They run their organizations like most other businesses. Sometimes they even run them better. And though the dividends are not measured in local currency, they are no less beneficial.

*   *   *

The People's Republic of Bangladesh has a population of approximately 150 million people, making it the seventh largest country in the world. With a per capita income that is well below US$1,000, it is one of the poorest as well. In 1940, Muhammad Yunus was born into a lower-middle-class family in Bangladesh. His parents had only finished elementary school, but they wanted their children to go to college. In 1961, Yunus graduated college in Bangladesh and became an economics teacher. In 1965, he received a Fulbright Scholarship to attend the University of Colorado and later received a Ph.D. in economics from Vanderbilt University. Returning to Bangladesh in 1972 after the country had won its independence, Yunus wanted to participate in rebuilding his nation. He ended up doing much more.

SOME ARE SAINTS

As head of the economics department at Chittagong University, in a rural part of Bangladesh, Yunus saw that the forty-two women in the local village of Jobra who made bamboo stools were caught in a vicious cycle of poverty. Each day they would go to a middleman who would sell them bamboo for $0.20 and then buy back from them a woven bamboo mat or stool for $0.22. These pennies were their only source of income, from which they had to feed their children and tend to their homes. They could not pay to send their children to school, meaning that the next generation would remain stuck in an unskilled vocation. But as bad as the conditions were for these women, it beat the 10 percent weekly interest rate the moneylenders would charge the women if they wanted loans to buy bamboo directly from local vendors and the freedom to sell their finished products to anyone. Yunus was determined to try to help. His initial goal was modest—help one person in the local village live a better life. He personally lent the villagers US$27 so that they could buy the bamboo themselves and sell their stools or mats in the marketplace to earn a higher return. His experiment worked. Since commercial banks lend money as their main business, Yunus visited the local bank to see if it would lend money to the women. He was disappointed when the bank manager told him that because the villagers were poor and had no collateral, it would be too risky to lend them money. The bank also said that lending such small amounts would be uneconomic for the banks since the administration of the loans would cost too much. Yunus argued that the very poor had no choice but to repay the loans because if they didn't, they could not get a loan the next day to buy the bamboo to make more mats and continue to earn their living. After six months Yunus finally persuaded the bank to lend the Jobra villagers the equivalent of US$300, provided that he personally guarantee the loan.

In January 1977 Yunus decided to start his own bank to provide very small loans to Bangladesh villagers. Yunus saw a huge potential to improve people's lives by breaking their connection to moneylenders and middlemen, who kept the poor villagers living at subsistence levels. His new institution, Grameen Bank, developed a program to give credit to the poor in a way that helped ensure repayment. By lending money to groups of people in a village rather than individuals, Grameen Bank created peer pressure among the borrowers—if any one of them missed a payment it might hinder subsequent loans across the village. In essence, the collective responsibility of the group served as the collateral for the loan. Since most of the villagers were illiterate, and since the paperwork normally associated with a loan was intimidating, Grameen did away with this requirement, only keeping a ledger of the transactions. Although Grameen Bank loans were tiny, they were adequate to meet the needs of the borrowers' very small businesses. The villagers used the money to buy livestock, rice-husking machines, textiles, and other raw materials. The loans were repayable weekly. If the borrowers were current on their loans they qualified for more. Bank employees visited the villages regularly, maintaining close contact with the borrowers and monitoring the progress with their businesses. Yunus also developed a series of very simple rules aimed to improve living and health conditions for the borrowers and their families. As a condition for loans the villagers had to agree to live by these rules.

Males dominate Bangladesh society, but Yunus learned quickly that lending money to women proved more efficient and effective because the women used any extra money to care for their children and homes, while the men were more apt to spend it on themselves. If Grameen Bank was to have a chance of reducing poverty in the villages it had to concentrate its loans on those people, women, who would improve the standard of living.

In June 1979 Yunus left the university to devote his time to developing the bank. At the time there were five hundred borrowers in Jobra village. Three years later, Grameen Bank had 28,000 borrowers in villages throughout Bangladesh, but getting there had not been easy. Many community groups were opposed to the notion of lending money to women. The men felt slighted and insulted, feeling that lending money to the women had weakened their authority in the household. Religious leaders also complained, suggesting that such loans violated religious codes. Political parties from the left complained that capitalism was sneaking into their country, and political parties from the right whined that it was a communist plot.

What made Grameen Bank distinctive in its fight against poverty was that its strategy was not about handouts or training, but was meant to help the people help themselves do what they already did. The approach did not impact their dignity, and it relieved their reliance on moneylenders and others that had oppressed them for so long. By giving villagers access to capital, albeit in very small amounts, Grameen Bank could move their lives forward.

To fund itself Grameen Bank takes in deposits, paying from 8 to12 percent annual interest, but it earns a spread by lending out money at interest rates of 20 percent on income-generating loans; 8 percent on housing loans; 5 percent on student loans, and 0 percent for its "struggling members" (beggars). Housing loans were introduced in 1984, with repayment over five years. The maximum housing loan is approximately US$350.[1] Approximately 58 percent of the families who have received Grameen Bank loans have moved out of poverty, and a World Bank study suggested that on average 5 percent of Grameen Bank borrowers rise out of poverty every year.[2,3]

From its humble beginnings in 1977, Grameen Bank has grown into a formidable institution and has become a model for microfinance ventures in numerous other countries. Today, Grameen Bank is owned primarily by its borrowers; the government of Bangladesh controls only 5 percent. Because Grameen Bank borrowers are also its owners, the interest payments on their loans do not violate the laws of Shariah (under Shariah law, such payments are not considered interest payments when the borrower is an owner). With approximately 25,000 employees operating from over 2,500 branches throughout the country, Grameen Bank services an estimated 8 million customers, 97 percent of whom are women. During this time, Grameen

Bank has disbursed over US$10 billion, 90 percent of which has been repaid; outstanding loans make up most of the difference. Grameen Bank now disburses over US$1 billion annually.

Given its established distribution network in rural villages and strong brand reputation with this customer group, Grameen Bank broadened its mission to leverage the foundation it had built. In 1996 Grameen Bank was awarded a cellular phone license to help bring modern communications to the villages. Establishing a for-profit subsidiary to build out the mobile phone network and a nonprofit subsidiary to sell phone time, Grameen Bank has become one of the largest communications companies in Bangladesh. Today, there are over 400,000 "phone ladies" who have the franchises for their villages. Following its success with mobile phones, Grameen Bank started a similar service to give villagers access to the Internet. And, with the need for electricity increasing, Grameen Bank has set up another subsidiary that works to bring "green energy," such as wind, biomass, and solar power, to villages as well.

Muhammad Yunus did not invent the idea of lending small amounts of money to the poor. The practice had started many hundred years earlier in other parts of the world. However, the large-scale success of Grameen Bank launched a massive movement for microfinance, which continues to grow. Approximately 100 million people around the world today access microcredit that is serviced by several thousand different groups, with a total estimated loan value topping US$36 billion. The success of the Grameen Bank earned the institution and its founder the Nobel Peace Prize in 2006. The borrowers of Grameen Bank and the other microfinance organizations that followed won a much bigger prize.

*   *   *

America in the late 1960s was rocked by turmoil and tension. Fallout from the escalating U.S. military activity in Vietnam brought people into the streets to protest the government's actions. Race riots in Detroit, Los Angeles, and Newark reflected a more aggressive civil rights movement and urban decay. The 1968 assassinations of Dr. Martin Luther King, Jr., and presidential candidate Robert F. Kennedy added to the notion of increasing violence in society. By contrast, in 1969 the Woodstock Music & Art Fair in upstate New York brought attention to the counterculture ethos of free love, marijuana, and rock 'n' roll music. It was protest in a different form. Against this backdrop emerged a revolutionary television show that would usher in a new and powerful educational approach that, in time, would nurture many generations of children around the globe and become a cultural landmark.

WHERE THE AIR IS SWEET

Joan Ganz was not your prototypical entrepreneur. After earning a degree in education from the University of Arizona in 1951, she worked her way to New York and got a job at NBC in the publicity department. A subsequent job with Channel 13, a small educational broadcasting station in New Jersey, exposed her to the production of documentaries and political shows. Ganz won an Emmy award in 1966 for her documentary on an adult literacy program called, "A Chance at the Beginning." To celebrate the milestone, her husband, Tim Cooney, held a party at their apartment. Among the guests was Lloyd Morrisett, vice president of the Carnegie Corporation, a nonprofit organization originally established by steel magnate Andrew Carnegie to promote education and understanding in the United States. At the time, the Carnegie Corporation was financing child-development research and funding numerous programs to help disadvantaged students. Morrisett knew that most three-to-five-year–olds would never go to preschool due to the lack of funds and space, and he wanted to find a way to reach them. Joan Ganz Cooney had an idea of how to make that happen.

When the Carnegie Corporation offered her $15,000 to research her ideas, Cooney went to work to determine how to use television to educate young children. She became an entrepreneur with a calling: using television to educate and thereby help alleviate poverty and ignorance. Common wisdom at the time said that television was a medium for entertainment and that the best children's education came from teachers in classrooms at their local schools. Children's television programming in those days mostly consisted of violent cartoons and a few morning programs, such as *Romper Room, Mister Rogers' Neighborhood*, and *Captain Kangaroo*.

At that time nearly all homes in the United States had television sets, and children were spending an average of twenty-seven hours per week in front of the box, even before they were old enough to go to school. Cooney's research indicated that young children retained much of what they saw on television, for example, easily remembering the commercials. In early 1968, she proposed to Morrisett that the Carnegie Corporation establish a nonprofit organization focused on using television to teach preschool education, and the Children's Television Workshop (CTW) was born. Its mission was to use modern entertainment techniques to engage preschool children and teach them basic subject matter.

Recognizing that her approach might encounter criticism from mainstream educators and child psychologists, Cooney set out to build a strong research base, and she collected inputs regarding preschooler curriculum from psychologists, teachers, and school officials. She spent eighteen months studying attention spans, areas of interest, and eye movements to better appreciate the needs of the expected audience. Cooney soon realized that unless her programming was entertaining as well as educational her target audience of young children would lose interest. To get the most out of the television medium, her team took a cue from the most popular television program in the country, *Rowan & Martin's Laugh-In*, a one-hour comedy show known for its fast-pace, short skits, and vibrant set colors. Cooney decided that her program should strive to teach young children simple counting ability, recognition of letters and numbers, some basic reasoning skills, simple vocabulary, and give them a greater sense of the world focusing on repetition, presentation, brevity, and clarity. These important perceptions reflected her background as a television producer, not an educator.

To create original programming for the first year of the show, to be called *Sesame Street*, Cooney needed $8 million. Like many entrepreneurs, she had to raise external funding to support the venture. Recognizing that for-profit television broadcasters would not provide financial assistance to a show aimed at preschoolers or reserve broadcast time for the target audience in the early morning or late afternoon, Cooney sought grants from the U.S. government and a variety of philanthropic organizations. Half of CTW's initial funding came from the United States Office of Education, which saw the potential for television to augment the Operation Head Start program. Incremental money came from the newly created Corporation for Public Broadcasting, the Carnegie Corporation, and the Ford Foundation.

To engage the preschool audience, Cooney's team wanted to tap into the creativity of Jim Henson's Muppets. Following in Walt Disney's footsteps, Henson had built a unique business around the puppet characters he had created. For CTW, Henson created several special characters, including Bert and Ernie, Oscar the Grouch, and Big Bird. Cooney set the show in an urban neighborhood, complete with tenements, garbage cans, and decay, and hired a cast that reflected the diversity of inner city life: a mix of Hispanic, black, and white actors, both men and women. In addition to developing distinctive programming, Cooney needed to build her audience. So she put together a nationwide campaign aimed at parents, to have their children watch the show. By broadcasting to public television stations across the country, Cooney charted new territory; traditionally, the programming on these channels targeted an affluent demographic interested in a dose of cultured entertainment.

Cooney signed up over one hundred educational TV stations around the country, and *Sesame Street* went live in November 1969. From the outset, the show was a huge success. In its first year, *Sesame Street* reached almost 7 million preschool children every day, five days a week. The show's "Rubber Ducky Song" was on the music charts for nine weeks, and several of the Muppet characters made guest appearances on adult-oriented television shows. *Sesame Street* also won three Emmys and two dozen other prizes for excellence in its first year.

When the Educational Testing Service studied children in five separate states in 1971 to understand whether the show's content was effective, they found that disadvantaged children who infrequently watched *Sesame Street* showed a general knowledge gain of 9 percent. Younger viewers who saw two or three shows a week jumped 15 percent; four or five viewings a week meant a 19 percent increase, and those who saw it more than five times weekly improved by 24 percent. The lower the age group, the better the show did, scoring its highest gains with three-year-olds.[4]

In 1972, CTW began to tap into the commercial power of its characters and to wean itself from foundation grants and government funding by setting up a marketing division. There were numerous opportunities for CTW to merchandise the Muppet characters, and they were looking to make a profit off these unique creations that they could then reinvest to fund program development. As Cooney explained, "The Muppets make us viable. I think had we not had Jim Henson and the Muppets, *Sesame Street* would have been successful in terms of popularity and acclaim, but I think it would have been a happy memory in two or three years. We would not have had this licensing program without Jim Henson. There is no doubt that a large part of the show's success can be attributed to him. For both Henson and us, it's been a wonderful marriage."[5]

Despite the naysayers, *Sesame Street* proved that a handful of thoughtful, imaginative people behind dedicated leadership could create high-quality, intelligent children's programming that entertains and teaches, better preparing them for the in-school experience. Moreover, *Sesame Street* established public broadcasting in the United States as a network that served a broad swath of the population, not only the affluent. Today, *Sesame Street* is viewed by almost half of all U.S. preschoolers on a weekly basis, and it has been broadcast in more than seventy-nine countries and twelve foreign-language versions around the world.

*   *   *

Yunus and Cooney created new businesses and opened new markets through processes similar to those used by for-profit entrepreneurs. They developed an idea, pulled together all the necessary pieces, and fashioned a venture out of whole cloth that most people thought would fail. Who would lend money to poor people? Who would use television to educate children? Time and time again, we see naysayers in the for-profit world. Sadly, we also see them in the nonprofit world. From an entrepreneurial perspective, the skills required to meet the challenge are pretty much the same. Grameen Bank and *Sesame Street* are only two of thousands of successful enterprises around the world in which social entrepreneurs make a big difference in people's lives through innovative solutions. While their rewards won't place them on the *Forbes 400*, they deserve at least equal adulation, support, and respect.

CHAPTER 12

ENTREPRENEURIAL GOVERNMENT

危机

*When written in Chinese, the word "crisis" is composed of two characters:
one represents danger, and the other represents opportunity.*
—John F. Kennedy

THE U.S. CONGRESS AND PRESIDENT DWIGHT D. EISENHOWER established the National Aeronautics and Space Administration (NASA) in 1958 to counteract the threat of Soviet domination of space following the launching in 1957 of Sputnik 1, the world's first artificial satellite. After Russian cosmonaut Yuri Gargarin's manned suborbital mission four years later, President John F. Kennedy boldly challenged America to put a man on the moon by the end of the decade—a goal the country successfully met with five months to spare. Human space flight galvanized the nation and pushed science and technology to new levels of achievement. However, it took presidential leadership to publicly prioritize the hefty expenditures necessary to develop the program. Fear was the great motivator, but "leadership" carried the day, setting the country on a targeted course with a specific goal and rationale.

Twenty-two years before JFK called on America to take action to protect itself in space, another president facing potential catastrophe boldly stepped up to lead the country in a high–risk, high-cost effort to end the war to end all wars. Like Kennedy, this president understood the responsibility and importance of getting in front, especially when the venture proves so hazardous.

CRISIS MANAGEMENT

Shortly before the German invasion of Poland ignited World War II on September 1, 1939, Albert Einstein alerted President Franklin D. Roosevelt to a possible threat to U.S. national security stemming from recent advances in nuclear physics made by European scientists. He told the president that the potential existed to construct a powerfully destructive bomb based on the chain reaction of uranium atoms. Einstein feared that Germany would develop this capability first and then use it for world domination. Recognizing the huge strategic advantage of owning such a potent weapon and the military signifi- cance of another nation getting an atomic bomb first, Roosevelt autho- rized the initial work to design a plan for the United States to build its own nuclear device. The pace of activity increased when, in July 1941, a report from scientists in England estimated that within two years, Germany would sufficiently improve the technology around uranium- 235 to produce an explosion.

No one had ever constructed such a device, but the U.S. govern- ment was prepared to throw significant resources at the problem to ensure that Germany did not get that advantage. In May 1942, a secret presidential task force evaluated the feasibility of several untried pro- cesses for manufacturing sufficient quantities of the critical uranium and plutonium isotopes needed to fuel a bomb. Roosevelt assigned the Army Corps of Engineers to build the atomic bomb, working from an office in New York City on what would become known as the Manhattan Project. The Army appointed forty-six-year-old Colonel Leslie R. Groves, who as the head of all the Army's U.S. building projects, had had over a million men working for him, to take charge of this highly secretive effort. Groves had recently overseen construc- tion of the world's largest office building, the Pentagon, and had been hoping for a combat assignment. Instead, he received the opportunity to dramatically alter the world.

Promptly promoted to Brigadier General, Groves went to work. He demonstrated superb leadership skills, establishing completion goals, marshalling resources, and recruiting experts to produce the explosive device as quickly as possible. With a large ego, a lack of charisma, and old-school taskmaster ways, Groves was not well-loved by those who worked for him, but he was highly respected for his intelligence, deci- siveness, and courage. He got things done.

In December 1942, at the University of Chicago, Nobel Prize-winning physicist, Enrico Fermi, who had immigrated to the United States from Italy in the 1930s, initiated the world's first self-sustaining chain reaction of uranium. That same month President Roosevelt authorized an incremental $500 million to the Manhattan Project, which had targeted the production of an atomic bomb by mid-year 1945. With Roosevelt's full support the U.S. government eventually spent over $2.2 billion on the effort to build the bomb.[1] Today, Roosevelt's expenditures appear warranted in light of the success of the project. But what if the effort to build the atomic bomb had failed? The political consequences would have been significant for FDR: the immense amount of money the government had spent trying to build the bomb could have supported the conventional military effort.

The need for speed and complete secrecy forced the Manhattan Project team to substantially amplify its risk. It took the highly unorthodox approach of skipping the normal multiyear time frame for scaling up similar chemical processes by short-circuiting the move from laboratory bench to full production. Given the huge number of technical uncertainties, including knowing which bomb-making technology would work and how much of each fissionable material was needed to fabricate a nuclear weapon, Groves decided to embark on four separate simultaneous development efforts, each requiring unprecedented effort and scale, with the hope that at least one approach would prove satisfactory for building the bomb in the desired time frame.

Under Groves's direction the U.S. government set about constructing three separate facilities. The first site was in Oak Ridge, Tennessee, which eventually employed 45,000 people, becoming the fifth largest city in the state. As the home of a massive building that was used to electromagnetically separate out specific uranium isotopes, it consumed nearly 15 percent of the nation's electricity. There were also facilities using gaseous diffusion and liquid thermal diffusion technologies. The second manufacturing site was located in Hanford, Washington, where the U.S. government efficiently acquired 500,000 acres of land and moved out 1,500 residents so it could move in 50,000 construction and plant workers dedicated to extracting plutonium. The third facility was built in Los Alamos, New Mexico, where 6,000 people, including the elite physicists of the day, worked in an isolated camp to build the nuclear device, which was fueled by materials made at the other sites.

Groves, in a highly controversial move, recruited Dr. J. Robert Oppenheimer, a thirty-nine-year-old professor from the University of California, Berkeley, to lead the efforts at Los Alamos. Oppenheimer was a brilliant theoretical physicist who had earned his Ph.D. at age twenty-two, spoke six languages, and had worked with many of the leading physicists in Europe and America. Importantly, Oppenheimer was not a Nobel laureate, as were several of the other scientists enticed to this remote locale and that he would have to manage. Oppenheimer described his success recruiting the necessary scientific talent:

> Almost everyone realized that this was a great undertaking. Almost everyone knew that if it were completed successfully and rapidly enough it might determine the outcome of the war. Almost everyone knew that it was an unparalleled opportunity to bring to bear the knowledge and art of science for the benefit of the country. Almost everyone knew that this job if it were achieved would be part of history.[2]

Oppenheimer had no managerial or administrative experience and was accused by one of his colleagues of lacking the skills to run a hamburger stand. Also, the FBI had him under regular surveillance as a potential security risk because he was alleged to have ties to the American Communist Party. Nonetheless, Groves's judgment proved to be exceptional. Oppenheimer excelled at his new responsibilities of overseeing the development effort and proved to be quite adept at motivating the scientists and administering the facility. He focused his efforts inside the laboratories, quietly coaxing the scientists and subtly influencing the direction of their work, but mostly showing presence and thoughtful participation at their formal meetings and informal discussions. Moreover, he shielded his civilian scientists from the hierarchical military protocols that would likely cramp their efforts.

Oppenheimer's greatest managerial challenge was to get his team of world-class physicists to evolve from conducting lab experiments to actually building something useful, a practicality most had never encountered before because they had never worked on a large-scale industrial engineering project. With few exceptions, they had come from environments in which they had been constrained by limited access to resources but had plenty of time to do their work. Now, they had limitless resources but felt tremendous pressure to meet the Manhattan Project's strict deadlines.

Groves and Oppenheimer effectively oversaw an extraordinary process of creating in a short period of time something that had never been done before. The scientists were under tremendous pressure and the stakes were extremely high. They produced the first weapon of mass destruction using untried science while coordinating colossal construction efforts across the country in total secrecy. At its peak the Manhattan Project employed nearly 130,000 people—approximately the size of the U.S. automobile industry at that time—and was costing $100 million a month.

During the winter of 1944, Oak Ridge had success with the electromagnetic isolation method, and later with the gaseous diffusion process for separating uranium-235. However, continued delays at Hanford delayed the delivery of purified plutonium to Los Alamos until February 1945. By early 1945, Oppenheimer declared finished the design of a uranium bomb that would shoot one piece of uranium-235 into another at very high velocity. When the uranium-235 combined, a nuclear explosion would (theoretically) occur. The scientists nicknamed the device Little Boy, and they had enough confidence in their work to conclude that it would not need testing. They had also designed a separate plutonium-fueled device that they expected to create a nuclear explosion by forcing a core of plutonium into a more compact, perfectly symmetrical mass in less than one millionth of a second. Less confident that the plutonium device, dubbed Fat Man, would work, Oppenheimer decided to test it.

On July 16, 1945, at a bombing range south of Los Alamos, scientists lifted the plutonium device, a kludgy contraption of metal and wires held together with screws and tape, to the top of a 100-foot steel tower. No one knew what might happen because in a dry run the day before with a blank charge the bomb had failed to fire. Some scientists voiced concern that a successful blast would ignite the atmosphere. But, when the bomb detonated as planned at 5:30 AM, the Atomic Age was born. Oppenheimer and his team had attained their goal in only twenty-seven months.

Following the detonation of the atomic bomb over Hiroshima, Japan, on August 6, 1945, President Harry S. Truman said of the Manhattan Project:

> The greatest marvel is not the size of the enterprise, its secrecy, nor its cost, but the achievement of scientific brains in putting together infinitely

complex pieces of knowledge held by many men in different fields of science into a workable plan. And hardly less marvelous has been the capacity of industry to design, and of the labor to operate, the machines and methods to do things never done before so that the brainchild of many minds came forth in physical shape and performed as it was supposed to do. Both science and industry worked under the direction of the United States Army, which achieved a unique success in managing so diverse a problem in the advancement of knowledge in an amazingly short time. It is doubtful if such another combination could be got together in the world. What has been done is the greatest achievement of organized science in history.[3]

In less than three years, Groves and Oppenheimer had successfully completed the largest scientific and engineering project in history. The introduction of the atomic bomb improved the power of weaponry on a scale that had never before been seen in the history of warfare. After the initial use of explosives, airplanes, tanks, long-range artillery, armor-clad warships, submarines, and rifles, it took years, and in some cases much longer, to feel their influence. It took only a few hours for the atomic bomb to transform military tactics and geopolitics while also setting the stage for harnessing a new source of energy to create electricity.

*   *   *

Many people around the world have a strong predisposition, often grounded in past experience, to believe that all governments—federal, state, and local—are incompetent bureaucracies staffed by indecisive people who blindly adhere to inflexible regulations. Government policy is often made by politicians with little experience in the real world who follow the whims of their constituencies and consistently sacrifice the long–term collective good to avoid an ounce of personal pain in the near term. The Manhattan Projection is an exception.

But in any new venture, the skills and approach of the entrepreneur set the stage for success or failure. Whether a project begins in a garage in Silicon Valley or as a massive federal government program, someone has to develop the conviction, take the initiative, and wield the power to get a positive outcome. The government proficiency demonstrated on the Manhattan Project rarely happens in the United States or elsewhere. Government has a unique ability to bring together unmatchable resources and focus them on the problems at hand. However, it often requires a crisis, and then it takes uncommon leadership at the top because of the high risks and the inevitable fallout in the event of failure. Someone has to step forth to take the upfront risk when such a decision may prove very unpopular, then expend the money, parry the inevitable adverse publicity, and enforce the agenda often expending their own political capital. FDR accomplished this objective with the Manhattan Project showing the tendencies and skills normally attributed to entrepreneurs. Behind General Groves's execution skills and J. Robert Oppenheimer's management style, the U.S. government, when it needed it most, demonstrated an unusual ability to rapidly turn a laboratory-style technology into a usable, albeit horrific, final product that substantially altered military weaponry and geopolitics, and laid the foundation for global nuclear power.

CHAPTER 13

GOVERNMENT MATTERS

Innovation has turned out to be a distinguishing characteristic of
the U.S. It is not simply invention; it is inventiveness put to use.
—Sir Harold Evans

IN THE BOOMING ECONOMIES OF THE DEVELOPING WORLD, INCLUDING
Brazil, China, India and eastern Europe, numerous entrepreneurs are
starting new businesses daily; some have already built mammoth enterprises. Their accomplishments are laudatory, but in most cases their
company's competitive advantage does not come from innovation, but
because they provide products and services at the lowest cost, accept
reduced profit margins, or have imported ideas that are already proven
elsewhere in the world; by definition they rely on a less defensible or
durable position than those with proprietary products and services.
Abundant entrepreneurial activity and recurrent innovation excellence
does not exist in a vacuum, nor does it materialize consistently without
the establishment of specific conditions. If a country's public-policy
goals aim for the long-term nurturing of systemic innovation and
entrepreneurship, then implementing a thoughtful multidimensional
mix of governmental policies that fit the cultural norms becomes vital.
Unfortunately, these conditions rarely coexist productively. As with
most things in life, off-the-shelf formulae infrequently provide one-
size-fits-all directions for reaching the intended objective. However,
the approach and lessons of those that have made significant headway
provide instructive examples of the art of the possible for building an
entrepreneurially driven economy. The different approaches pursued
and implemented by the United States, Israel, and China provide infor-
mative perspective.

MADE IN AMERICA

America, a nation born out of rebellion and founded by people who were prepared to make the ultimate sacrifice, has contributed a disproportionate share of the world's entrepreneurial energy since the late nineteenth century, formulating transformative innovations based on new business models and leading-edge technologies. Although dozens of other nations have won independence from colonial powers through popular uprisings, many lacked the all-important next step for long-term economic prosperity: a system of government that fosters liberty, ensures protection of property, and enforces rule of law. The U.S. Constitution ratified in 1789 and amended by the Bill of Rights in 1791 may rate as the world's most impressive "innovation," if not the pinnacle of human intellect applied to the most inexact of all sciences—government. The Constitution gave America a political system that supported and cultivated capitalism without which an entrepreneurial wellspring could not emerge. Government policies and regulations provide an extremely important, almost decisive, foundation for the entrepreneurial activity that drives innovation because it creates both the potent incentives and constricting constraints that impact new company formation.

Liberty proved to be the most powerful of magnets, attracting a constant flow of immigrants, and continually infusing the country with new energy and the new ideas that provide the lifeblood of an innovation economy. Andy Grove, retired CEO and Chairman of Intel and its third employee, who came to America as a poor immigrant from Hungary, once said: "Friends told me that all I needed was ability. Americans don't know how lucky they are."[1] While it would be a gross overstatement to claim that America is a pure meritocracy, compared to most other places, it is. For those with self-confidence and the requisite skills, living in a meritocracy offers huge attraction. By their nature immigrants are risk takers, courageous pioneers who tend to appreciate freedom more than most. And, they come with new notions and cultural norms that broaden and strengthen the existing society over time. In short, they provide a great feedstock of entrepreneurs.

Another of America's distinguishing attractions has been the breadth and quality of its universities and colleges. Although the United States' education system struggles to maintain global competitiveness in its elementary schools and high schools, its many top-ranked universities with excellent facilities and foremost professors draw some of the brightest students from around the world, who initially come to get a top-notch education, and then stay because the opportunities for employment have tended to be greater than in their home lands. America, from its founding days, understood the benefits of welcoming those from other countries, endowing itself with the attributes of independence, nearly level playing field, higher education, and optimism that appeals to the top strata from afar.

But immigration explains only part of America's success. The country additionally supports entrepreneurs through a well-defined legal system which enforces a strong rule of law. In the eighteenth century the authors of the U.S. Constitution presciently added provisions regarding intellectual property and bankruptcy to help protect those who were willing to take risks, thereby providing a further incentive to take risk in the first place. And, specifically with respect to bankruptcy, the regulatory framework that emerged over subsequent years outlines a pathway for those who try but fail to get a fresh start without too many encumbrances or waste of resources.

In the mid-1970s Congress changed the laws to allow pension funds, among America's largest and fastest growing pools of capital, the flexibility to devote a portion of their assets toward investment in more risky arenas, which has fueled the formation and scale of venture capital, and other investment pools that finance corporate growth. The added funds helped shape the venture capital model which supports entrepreneurs at the early stages of company formation and growth. Fully-formed and highly regulated public equity markets allow the investors that have provided the early stage capital to realize the value they created while providing access to lower cost capital for continued growth. A tax structure that encourages investment by providing lower tax rates on capital gains and rules that permit employees to benefit from stock options further buttresses the foundation.

Government has played another important role as a leading investor in research and development, especially in areas of technology, including pharmaceuticals, military applications, computer hardware and software, advanced materials, and alternative energy. Through programs administered by such institutions as the National Institute of Health, the Defense Advanced Research Projects Agency (DARPA), and NASA substantial financial support goes into the private sector, including many emerging growth companies, and to research groups often affiliated with universities and national laboratories. Federal government largesse comes with billion-dollar outlays which have become increasingly important over the years as large corporations have curtailed expenditure on research to focus instead on product development because it offers quicker paybacks. The U.S. government spent approximately $150 billion on research-related activities in 2010. Long-term, however, economies and technology-oriented entrepreneurs need consistent programs of fundamental and applied research to achieve the scientific advances and inventions that will create innovation opportunities. Without investment to move the frontiers of science and technology that expand the knowledge base, the world's ability to consistently improve living standards likely will stagnate over time. Competitively, the nations that fall behind in this important category will lag as well.

Culturally, as much as Americans love to root for the underdog, they love winners even more. And, the winners they respect most are those who started with little and then made something of themselves—successful entrepreneurs. Even self-proclaimed nerds like Bill Gates and Mark Zuckerberg emerged as role models for would-be entrepreneurs, idolized for their cutting-edge achievements. Plenty of proofpoints of the accomplishments of those who create innovative businesses are publicized, though far fewer than warranted—especially compared with the headlines granted to movie stars, politicians, and criminals—to demonstrate the attractiveness of entrepreneurial success.

Mixed together, these traits and forces have endowed the United States with a unique blend of attributes that facilitate new businesses based on innovative technologies and approaches, and encourage individuals to step out and try to do something that has proven very difficult to achieve. It is impossible to assess which of these many factors most enables entrepreneurial development and innovation; it is the uncommon combination that makes it work.

THE LAND OF DAVID

Many countries see great opportunity to develop their own entrepreneurial communities and foster innovation by replicating the U.S. venture capital model. But, this combination is so rare and hard to implement, even over long periods of time, it seems unlikely that other countries could copy it and get the same impact if they wanted to. While other countries may replicate some of the conditions that underpinned the United States' achievement, don't expect too many successes because the requisite attributes need to work harmoniously for a positive end result; a tall order.

Interestingly, Israel, with a population of less than 8 million people and plenty of geopolitical challenges, stands out as the country with the most developed venture capital industry in the world for its size and economic scale. In 2010 Israeli venture capital investment exceeded $1.2 billion, ranking it as the highest amount of any nation as a function of GDP, more than double the level of the United States. Israeli-based companies are the third largest source of NASDAQ-listed entities, trailing only the United States and Canada. How has this small nation with a constant state of political turmoil and national stress given its hostile borders managed to develop a prosperous entrepreneurial community as well as an extremely strong technology base?

Numerous studies and articles have tried to explain what makes Israel so successful, including most recently Daniel Senor and Saul Singer's 2009 book *Start-Up Nation: The Story of Israel's Economic Miracle*. The explanations suggest a multitude of government actions combined with some unusual cultural traits magnified by some basic tenets of an entrepreneurial community. The overlap of themes with the United States' success in this area should come as no surprise.

First, the Israeli government has made it a priority to create an attractive climate for entrepreneurship and risk taking, at least compared to most governments, recognizing early on that this pathway of encouraging early stage ventures was the best way to spur sustainable lasting employment and economic growth. Taking a page from the United States' Small Business Administration's programs, in 1993 Israel helped jump-start a venture capital industry, earmarking $100 million of government funds to support new businesses. By providing matching funds to venture capital firms, the government helped to leverage a small capital base into something more meaningful. With access to less expensive capital new venture capital firms formed providing a helpful resource for the entrepreneurial community. More recently, Israel has provided grants for small companies in approximately twenty-three incubators around the country. This approach has fostered more cooperation and shared support for embryonic businesses.

Second, the Israeli military has a long history of funding new technology recognizing the need to leverage its relatively small armed forces with more advanced weaponry than possessed by its neighbors.

Moreover, and perhaps most important, the military has a command philosophy of delegating decision-making authority down the ranks to "twenty-somethings," which has the added benefit of creating more self-confident leaders when it comes time to start a business. Programs that select candidates to join several elite units within the Israeli Defense Forces also serve to establish strong bonds and trust among the countries best and brightest, who, upon leaving the military developed a tradition of forming their own companies and have a network in place for accessing many of the country's most talented individuals.

Third, as a land of immigrants, especially from the former Soviet Union, Israel has benefited from an influx of well-educated, risk-taking, new arrivals eager to participate in the economy. As with the United States, a consistent flow of immigrants has provided an important stream of would-be entrepreneurs with a different mindset than most when it comes to starting their own companies. Further, Israeli culture tolerates failure in its start-up companies and does not penalize entrepreneurs who try but fail. In fact, it has become part of the business tradition to start ones' own business because the nation sees entrepreneurship as an important contributor to economic growth, prosperity and security.

Fourth, Israelis value education, especially higher education. Twenty-four percent of its workforce has a university degree, a number that is bested only by The Netherlands and the United States. Israel also has the leading percentage of engineers per capita, with levels nearly double the United States and Japan.

THE BIG RED MACHINE

The means and methods, assets and approaches that have stimulated innovation and entrepreneurship in the United States and Israel may not work as well in other places. China, with its 1.3 billion population, has grown its economy at an average high-single-digit annual rate over the past ten years, exhibiting tremendous new business activity and energy without the positive forces at work that partially explain the previous two examples: meaningful foreign immigration, intellectual property protection, bankruptcy regulations, political tolerance, consistent enforcement of rule of law, or a well-oiled venture capital ecosystem. The strong revenue and profit growth of the leading Chinese companies primarily reflects the conversion of state-owned enterprises from a more socialist to a capitalist economic system, extremely low cost government-supplied capital, massive migration, measured in the hundreds of millions of people into urban centers from rural areas, and a mercantilist approach to international business. But, China is rapidly changing some parts of this equation recognizing that its economy remains vulnerable if low-cost manufacturing alone has to carry the burden. The programs to transition the economy and entrepreneurial pursuits to high value-added content already are falling into place, which has profound implications for twenty-first century economic power.

Most Chinese companies are not yet growing based on pioneering technologies or new inventions. But, foreign multinationals have taken aggressive steps to increase their worldwide product development focus with increasingly large offices and research facilities in China. In time, as these centers gain experience they will introduce new technologies and products that provide the basis for innovation and more entrepreneurial activity. As China's university system matures and multiplies to support a greatly expanding student body, it should pay off with more talent, especially in producing engineering, science and math-trained graduates who will form the backbone of the workforce. This added focus on training and facilitating research and development skills, and the ability to generate proprietary intellectual property may, over time, shift the country's bias from one of appropriating others' insights and creativity to defending this important and valuable asset. With the country's financial system evolving quickly, including its stock exchanges, sovereign wealth funds and rapidly proliferating venture capital sector, the capital resources necessary to support the formation and growth of new enterprises will likely flourish, as will the experience set of home-grown entrepreneurs and investors with an appetite for risk. Already, China's abundance of funds supplies plentiful inexpensive capital to new businesses, and a stated policy for cultivating Chinese ventures at the expense of foreign corporations deters competition allowing the local companies to buy time to establish themselves, gain scale and experience before facing the intensity of the more established international challengers anxious to penetrate the world's most important long-term market.

Lastly, and maybe most importantly, the government control of the Chinese economy, which targets certain industrial sectors for high growth, translates into considerable government subsidies to ensure that industries deemed strategic for the long term, such as cleantech, health care, and IT, get more than their fair share of resources. These subsidies may be in the form of lower tax rates, free real estate, relaxed environmental and labor laws compared to international standards, and access to low-cost funding. Together, the package enables new companies to develop significant competitive advantages, and the playing field gets slanted meaningfully in their direction. Over time, with plenty of experience, leading-edge skills, an abundance of entrepreneurial role models, and considerable financial resources and regulatory advantages the country expects to have in place all of the necessary conditions for a broad-based innovation engine.

*   *   *

America, Israel, and China offer three different vintages and vantages for establishing an entrepreneurial economy each reflective of their origins, resources, politics, and cultures. Their government policies and philosophies, initiatives, and leadership have each set the stage, albeit distinctly, for engendering this important component for driving economic growth, improving living standards, and enabling technological advantage. To the extent that the other nations of the world want to compete on the same playing field, they will need to promote their own combination of regulations and incentives or risk being left behind, with all of the political and economic consequences.

CHAPTER 14

INNOVATE OR DIE

Carpe diem.
—Horace

THE DRIVE FOR INNOVATION HAS NEVER BEEN GREATER THAN it is today. The topic permeates corporate board rooms, business school classrooms, sovereign-wealth and municipal-pension-fund investment committees, government policy meetings on tax codes, immigration quotas, spending programs, and education reform. The discussion takes place at all levels, all around the world: individuals, private-sector enterprises, and philanthropic organizations. Every one of these groups has the need and desire to keep from getting stale and hopes to open up new possibilities for expansion and improvement. They all recognize that in an increasingly competitive world, standing still is tantamount to giving up. It is not an option.

WELCOME TO THE INNOVATION AGE

Since the late eighteenth century, historic advances in technology have ushered in five distinct economic revolutions, each spurring step-function improvements in the standard of living of those countries fortunate enough to enjoy and deploy these breakthroughs. The First Industrial Revolution began in 1771 when the advent of Arkwright's water-powered textile mill brought mechanization and factory automa-tion to a hand-made world. The "Rocket" steam locomotive in 1829 initiated the second industrial revolution, propelling Britain to the forefront of global economic leadership. The age of steel and electric-ity produced by Andrew Carnegie's steel plant and Thomas Edison's numerous inventions for producing and using electricity commencing in the mid-1870s started a third: the transition to American economic leadership, and a tremendous leap forward in the standard of living. The fourth was the age of oil and automobiles, primarily initiated by Henry Ford's Model T in 1908, which furthered the United States manufacturing-led prowess that carried through World War II and beyond. The Information Age, also commercialized first in the United States, that began in the early 1970s with the introduction of Intel's microprocessor and was supplemented by inventions in optoelectronics, fiber optics, and computer software led the transformation to a postindustrial economy in which services outstripped manufacturing, and knowledge workers have replaced factory labor. The Internet, an outgrowth of the fifth wave of technology advancement, moved from academic, military, and scientific networks in the 1980s to become a commercial powerhouse in the mid-1990s. Today, it forms the primary backbone supporting the current wave of innovation. With the construction of new applications still in the early innings, both for consumers and businesses, Internet-enabled services herald even greater fortunes ahead by continuing to attract tremendous entrepreneurial activity all over the world, and massive corporate spending on new product and services development that will exploit the shifting living, communications, and purchasing practices of the populace.

The technology breakthroughs behind each of these revolutions were not obvious or foreseeable much before they happened. Although such breakthroughs are not pre-announced, they seem to come about every fifty years or so, igniting an entirely new round of improvements and a step-change in the global economy that is mostly fostered by entrepreneurs who carry little baggage in terms of rigid business models, existing businesses to protect, or organizational silos.

Each technology-led revolution over the past two hundred and fifty years has had a profound impact on society, lifting productivity, improving efficiencies, and leading to radical reductions in the cost structures of associated goods and services. The cornerstone technologies that instigated each of these revolutions unleashed over the subsequent thirty to forty years a constant flow of disruption to the way people worked and lived, as innovators learned how to harness these new tools and create new business models, and encouraged governments to invest in new infrastructure.

Although each technology revolution got its start in one locale the businesses spawned subsequently spread to other countries and markets. The pace of proliferation has quickened over the years, perhaps minimizing the competitive advantage for the original host country, but increasing the potential for global market shares and higher profitability for those companies that climbed aboard quickly or developed the meaningfully superior product offering. However, protection of intellectual property, especially transborder, looms today as the elephant in the room because without such protection the incentive to create new technologies will vanish quickly. Those who foot the bill will retrench, uncomfortable about taking on the upfront risk if others around the world usurp the gain.

Not surprisingly, the euphoria and excitement that followed the introduction of many of these new technologies, especially railroads, automobiles, and the Internet, gave rise to exuberance in the financial markets, with investors projecting wholesale overhauls of old industries far in advance of reality. From a societal perspective these bubbles were not totally destructive; they had desirable side-effects that resulted in the availability of large quantities of cheap capital to support entrepreneurial activity. While many speculators ended up with little to no return on investment after each bubble deflated, society benefited because the funding they contributed financed the hard assets that remained in place, such as the fiber-optic communications network, and numerous successful companies that became leaders in new markets and trailblazers for the future.

Whereas technology revolutions consistently have spurred entrepreneurial activity launching disruptive innovations, many new business models that are not driven by novel inventions but solely from novel ideas emerge. Changing government regulations, shifting demographics, or economic dislocations frequently provide the catalyst that generates the opportunity for new businesses where entrepreneurs with vision and skill can make things happen. Increasingly, as a successful business in one part of the world becomes broadly known, local entrepreneurs adapt it for their regions or specific market conditions, such as Ryanair's duplication of Southwest Airlines' strategy for Europe, and then AirAsia following suit in southeast Asia, and more recently, the formation of Azul in Brazil to bring low-cost air transportation to this region.

The enabling technologies of the Information Age leveled the global business terrain, realigning or diminishing the competitive advantages of many mature companies. In a world that is connected through a broadband Internet and mushrooming social networks, information flows quickly and relatively seamlessly, expediting the pace at which new innovations gain traction and spread. For example, the companies that have historically delivered information and entertainment content in "printed" form, such as newspapers, books, music CDs, and movie DVDs, are the most obvious examples of endangered species as they increasingly face pressure from services that deliver the same content digitally. Conversely, for those nimble and brave enough to run toward the cutting edge, such as Google, Netflix, Apple, and Amazon.com—note the long-term presence of their entrepreneurial founders—the embodiment of Schumpeter's "creative destruction" plays out.

GRAND ILLUSION

America has never had a monopoly on brains, though at various points in the recent past the United States has held leadership positions in capital flows, various consumer and industrial markets, leading-edge technologies, functioning distribution channels, skilled labor, investment in research and development, many manufacturing sectors, and managerial processes. Although it retains top-tier status in per capita GDP among the major economies of the world, as globalization has begun to flatten the world and ushered in cross-fertilization of ideas, "best practices" transfers, and economic evolution in both the developed and the developing countries, many of those leadership positions have vanished or weakened considerably, and in some cases they will never return. Moreover, although still powerful, Western companies and entrepreneurs, including those located in the United States, no longer control the innovation agenda unilaterally; there is a much broader and richer mix of participants who are ever desirable and capable of carving out their coveted niche.

A 2009 report by the World Economic Forum stated,

> In the long run, standards of living can be expanded only with innovation...Firms...must design cutting-edge products and processes to maintain a competitive edge. This requires an environment that is conducive to innovative activity supported by both the public and the private sectors. In particular, this means sufficient investment in research and development, the presence of high-quality scientific research institutions, extensive collaboration in research between universities and industry, and the protection of intellectual property.[1]

It also means that regulatory policies to promote and accommodate immigration, improve educational systems, and enable smooth functioning capital markets, especially risk capital, must move up on the political "to do" list.

Many people today question America's future leadership role in the world economy. They focus on the inadequacies of its public education system, its gridlocked and polarizing political partisanship, hollowed-out manufacturing base, the short-term greed of Wall Street's financial engineers, the litigiousness of society, and a broader cultural sloth and lack of accountability, all set against a backdrop of the emergence and growing political and economic power of the newly hungry economies. The escalating fear of foreign oil dependency, anthropomorphic climate change, international terrorism, and nuclear proliferation compound the sense that as a world power and economic giant America has peaked and can go in only one direction. They predict the fall of the American Empire.

Although some pundits loudly proclaim that the end is near, most likely it is not. The United States has a long history excelling at innovation and entrepreneurship, and these attributes should provide one key to the nation's ability to maintain competitiveness and support a growing economy compared with the increasing number of countries around the world that have embraced democracy and learned to exploit capitalism. The curvy path ahead has potholes and speed bumps, placing an added burden on the entrepreneurs and business leaders who volunteer to show us the way, but a small dose of optimism grounded in history portends a bright future.

History suggests that another wave of formative technology will emerge from the shadows within the next decade or so taking the worldwide economy to a new level of performance. The source of the original ideas and inventions may come from anywhere. But, America, culturally, academically, and commercially maintains an extremely strong position, with the entrepreneurial bench strength to rapidly commercialize this creativity, homegrown or otherwise, into full-blown, industrial-sized innovation, multiply it across numerous business sectors, and reap the benefits.

PASSION PLAY

Now is a great time to be an entrepreneur nearly anywhere on the globe. With a long litany of problems to solve, the world offers huge potential for those anxious to make their mark. Pick your favorite: global warming, potable water availability, energy supply, health care, computer security, education reform, alternative fuels, and so many others. With technology advancing at an increasing rate and product-development cycles continually compressing, fresh ideas emerge regularly for how to harness new tools and deploy them to create exciting companies in such diverse areas as pharmaceuticals, bionics, space travel, speech recognition, cloud computing, digital media, wireless communications, photovoltaics, biofuels, and advanced materials.

Outside the technology-driven arena ample opportunities ripen daily awaiting some person or some company to take the plunge, push the envelope, and not get sidetracked by fear of failure. In the developed world, whole industries, such as financial services, travel, information services, logistics, and health-care services, stand ready for renovation. In fact, most business sectors would benefit greatly from modernization on a recurrent basis. We see this repeatedly in new restaurant and retailing concepts, and in fashion and entertainment, but the manufacturing and other service segments of the economy have much to gain from inventive approaches to meeting the evolving needs and tastes of their customers. For the emerging economies, innovative new businesses may take tried-and-true concepts from Europe or America and tailor them for the local markets, or introduce homegrown ideas, taking advantage of native customs and resources; examples include the proliferation of fast-food restaurants in eastern Europe, the very low-cost automobiles manufactured in India, and sugar cane-based ethanol production in Brazil. More broadly, new business themes that revolve around enhanced customer self-service; the sharing of assets, such as Netflix DVDs or Vélib' bicycles in Paris; social enterprises; shifting demographics; conservation; and the recycling of used resources all provide ample running room for entrepreneurial input and leadership.

Surprisingly, the availability of money to support entrepreneurial activity has rarely been a limiting factor in the United States over the past thirty years. Instead, the quantity of high–quality management teams and attractive business models attacking sufficiently large markets has set the pace. As long as global capital markets remain flush and interest rates stay near historical lows, the funding required to build and grow companies abounds. This does not mean that anyone can raise large amounts of capital to launch their favorite idea or pet project, but for attractive opportunities in North America, and increasingly in parts of Europe, India, China, Brazil, and beginning now in Africa quality management teams should find adequate financial support from venture capitalists and angel investors. Assuming that the experience set for backing new businesses continues to expand in the developing world, funding processes will become more fluid while funding levels grow.

*   *   *

The beauty of watching talented entrepreneurs at work stems from their optimism and enthusiasm. They love what they do and they want you to love it too. All the entrepreneurs cited in this book, both those who succeeded and those who fell short, combined intuitive understanding, great desire, and a 24/7 commitment. It is what made them entrepreneurs, anxious and willing to go out on the limb to lead from the front. They wouldn't want it any other way, and they probably could not have controlled themselves anyway.

Tolstoy said, "Ideas that have great results are always simple ones." In reality, sometimes they are very complicated or nuanced, but great results only come from steadfast implementation of the idea, regardless of complexity. It is not the idea, in and of itself, that distinguishes the great entrepreneurs; it is what they do with the idea. It is their actions over a period of time to mold, shape, and adjust the idea, to tune it and fine-tune it and then wrap the full swath of business disciplines around it. As Henry Ford once observed, "Vision without execution is just hallucination."

Outstanding execution begins with great leadership. It starts at the top of any organization, whether it is two guys in a garage pursuing a start-up, the fancy corner office of a multinational enterprise, the dimly lit spaces with cracked linoleum floors of a growing business in an emerging economy, or in the ornate halls of government. Someone has to step forth to filter the best ideas, command the necessary resources, accept the risks, and then cause things to happen. Innovation success comes when someone correctly makes most of the thousands of little decisions involved in getting an enterprise off of the ground, and combines that with superhuman heroic perseverance. Big companies can introduce major innovations, but someone senior in the organization has to play the role of the entrepreneur, cutting through the bureaucracy, incentivizing those further down in the company to take the risk, but not unduly punishing failed attempts. The same leadership requirement applies to government processes. Those in positions of power need to take the political risk to coax and cajole fellow legislators and voting constituencies.

Plenty of people around the globe today are smart, enthusiastic, confident, and hungry to succeed. They have their eyes and imaginations wide open, on the lookout for new opportunities, sifting through unparalleled information flows, with access to more tools and experience than ever before. Abraham Lincoln said, "Things may come to those who wait, but only the things left by those who hustle." Gifted entrepreneurs know how to hustle, and when they dream big, transformative innovation ensues.

ACKNOWLEDGMENTS

THE IDEA BEHIND THIS BOOK COMES FROM MY TEACHINGS at Columbia University's Graduate School of Business, a storied institution that let a novice take control of one of its classrooms and try to meet the expectations of its tuition-paying students. Fortunately, the experiment has worked well enough, though I often learned more than I taught. I owe these MBA students for their contribution to this book because without them it would never have happened. My primary Columbia Business School connection, Professor Murray Low, Director of the Entrepreneurship Program, started me down this path and then kept me on course reminding me to crawl before trying to walk. Columbia CaseWorks, the business case publishing group of Columbia Business School, published much of my original courseware, including several case studies on topics used in this book. I appreciate their help and editorial guidance.

Laurie Harting, Executive Editor at Palgrave Macmillan, had the courage to support this project and then provided the soft touch and wisdom of a professional to enforce a coherent structure while rounding the jagged edges of my prose. Sir Harold Evans, author of the award-winning *They Made America*, graciously spoke to one my classes, bringing alive the stories of people who were so important to moving this country forward. His book served as an anchor for this work and a catalyst for many of its themes. I am also grateful to Christo and Jeanne-Claude, who visited my class and engaged the students with their unique perspective.

Nearly my entire business career has been spent in the world of venture capital where I enjoy a regular diet of entrepreneurs and dreamers, businessmen and women, bonded by the common theme that they want to bring their fresh ideas to fruition. From the worlds of information technology, communications, energy, consumer goods and industrial products the flood of people looking for capital to help achieve their ambitions runs constantly; a seemingly never-ending waterfall. Even when their skills are sometimes limited, their optimism is infectious. Their glass is never half empty even when the water is gone. They inspire. Fortunately, some succeeded making those of us that financed them look smart.

My many colleagues at Warburg Pincus, where I have worked for the past twenty-eight years, contributed the judgment, wisdom, and excellent investment skills that provided me with the livelihood to spend a career interfacing with the entrepreneurial class. I owe special thanks to my long-time partners Bill Janeway and Henry Kressel for their enlightened perspective on historical times and explaining what they all meant.

If I am spending time researching and writing a book, then something else isn't getting done or someone else isn't getting my time and attention. Usually that someone was a family member or a business partner or one of my favorite philanthropies. I can call my educational work a hobby or a leisure activity and try to explain away the distraction from my primetime constituencies, but I know that others were very patient and understanding to allow me this luxury. Until my children grew up and adventured off to college I did not have the time to pull together the material to write this book. I was sad to see them go, jealous of their opportunity, and always excited when they returned. Rachel and Daniel make me proud to be their father.

And, the best for last, my wife, Jamie—who has weathered all of the storms and the countless business trips while I pursued my career aspirations—deserves undying gratitude as the one constant in my ever-changing and never dull universe.

JEFFREY A. HARRIS
New York, 2011

Notes

Introduction

1. *American Heritage Dictionary of the English Language* New York: American Heritage Publishing Co., Inc. 1969
2. T.R. Reid, *The Chip: How Two Americans Invented The Microchip and Launched A Revolution.* New York: Random House, 1985.
3. www.thomasedison.com/quotes.html.
4. Joseph Schumpeter, *Business Cycles: A Theoretical, Historical, and Statistical Analysis of the Capitalist Process.* New York: McGraw-Hill Book Company, 1939.
5. dictionary.com 2011.
6. Robert Sobel, *The Entrepreneurs: An American Adventure.* Boston: Houghton Mifflin, 1986. p. ix
7. Peter F. Drucker, *Innovation and Entrepreneurship: Practice and Principles,* New York: Harper Collins 1985 p. 19
8. Some people credit Winston Churchill with this quotation.
9. *They Made America.* WGBH Boston. Video 2004.
10. http://www.goodreads.com/author/quotes/203714.Henry_Ford.

1 Changing the Landscape

1. Albert Maysles, dir. *Christo & Jeanne-Claude: 5 Films,* Maysles Film Production, 2004.
2. Felda Hardymon, Josh Lerner, and Ann Leamon. "Christo and Jeanne-Claude: The Art of the Entrepreneur" Harvard Business School Press, case 9-806-014 [revised], August 7, 2006.
3. Steven Watts, *Mr. Playboy: Hugh Hefner and the American Dream,* Hoboken, NJ: John Wiley & Sons, 2008, 44.
4. Ibid., 55.
5. Ibid., 52.
6. Ibid., 70.
7. Ibid., 82.

8. Louis B. Parks, "Hugh Hefner's Playboy Magazine Turns 50," *Houston Chronicle,* December 14, 2003.

2 CREATIVE CONSTRUCTION

1. H.W. Brands, *Masters of Enterprise: Greats of American Business, from John Jacob Astor and J.P. Morgan to Bill Gates and Oprah Winfrey,* New York: The Free Press, 1999, 106.
2. Neil Gabler, *Walt Disney: The Triumph of the American Imagination,* New York: Vintage Books 2006, 632.

3 TRUE GRIT

1. Federal Express launched a television advertising campaign effectively using humor to its advantage. "America, you've got a new airline, the first major airline in over 30 years. No first class, no meals, no movies – in fact, no passengers, just packages. Small important shipments that have to get where they're going overnight, and up to now have had to fly at the mercy of the passenger airlines. Not anymore. Federal Express – a whole new airline for packages only." Subsequent ads won numerous awards including a series with its "absolutely, positively overnight service" slogan.
2. Fred Smith, 1998. Interview by Academy of Achievement Website, May 23, http://www.achievement.org/autodoc/page/smi0int-1
3. UHF (ultra high frequency) transmission of television signals allowed use of smaller antennae for broadcasting signals but only reached smaller broadcast areas. Used in the early days of television, the stations that utilized this technology tended to be unaffiliated with the major networks (ABC, CBS, and NBC), had smaller budgets, and were less polished than those using VHF (very high frequency) signals.
4. Harold Evans, *They Made America: From The Steam Engine to the Search Engine Two Centuries of Innovators,* New York: Little, Brown and Company, 2004, 586.

4 NEW HORSES FOR OLD COURSES

1. *American Made,* CNBC, April 17, 2006. Burrelles Luce.
2. Ibid.
3. Howard Schultz and Dori Jones Yang. *Pour Your Heart Into It: How Starbucks Built a Company One Cup at a Time,* New York: Hyperion, 1997, p. 160–161.

4. *American Made: Howard Schultz*, CNBC April 17, 2006. Burrelles Luce

5   NEXT-MOVER ADVANTAGE

1. Southwest Airlines positioned itself as the "fun" airline, often taking advantage of its use of Love Field in Dallas in its advertising slogans: "The 48-Minute Love Affair," "At last, there's somebody up there who loves you," and "Love Can Change Your Ways." Other slogans were "A Fare To Remember" and "At Last a $20 Ticket You Won't Mind Getting."
2. Southwest Airlines started throwing parties on board its aircraft with birthday cakes and balloons for passengers. In addition, they created a club for executive secretaries and awarded them free trips when they made a certain number of reservations on the airline. As competition increased Southwest began offering lower fares, such as $10 on selected routes at selected times.

6   FAILURE IS AN OPTION

1. John Heilemann, "Machine of Dreams", *Vanity Fair,* May 2002, 224.
2. Segway Inc. buyer, Jim Heselden, died in September 2010 in an accident while riding a ruggedized Segway at his estate in the United Kingdom. Apparently, he drove over a cliff and crashed into the river below.
3. In August 1974, Malcolm Bricklin, a young entrepreneur who had made millions of dollars importing Subarus, engineered an arrangement with the Canadian government to begin producing a new two-seat car that had gull wing doors. The company made 3,000 vehicles before closing down.

7   BAD BOYS

1. This quotation usually is attributed to film producer Samuel Goldwyn
2. Napster agreed to block the file sharing of artists who did not want their music shared.

8   ENTERPRISING ENTERPRISES

1. Western Union Telegraph Company internal letter. November 15, 1876
2. *The New York Times*, April 21, 1939 p.16.
3. Robert Cringely (writer/producer). 1996. *The Triumph of the Nerds: The Rise of Accidental Empires;* Episode 3.

4. David Owen, "Copies In Seconds," *The Atlantic Monthly,* February 1986, 67.
5. The Altair 8800 was made by MITS, a small Albuquerque, New Mexico, electronics company.
6. Cringely, *Nerds.*

9   THE EPITOME OF INNOVATION

1. Johnson became CEO of J.C. Penney in 2011.
2. Examples include Lisa and PowerMac G4 Cube personal computers, the MobileMe cloud-based storage system for remote access of files, and Apple TV.

10   VENTURESOME CAPITAL

1. Alex Ayres, ed. *The Wit and Wisdom of Mark Twain.* New York: New American Library 1987.

11   NOBLE ENDEAVORS

1. www.grameen.com
2. Transcript of session on "Ending Global Poverty" with Muhammad Yunus hosted by Isobel Coleman of the Council on Foreign Relations, New York, New York November 16, 2006
3. Shahidur R. Khandker, 1998. *Fighting Poverty with Microcredit: Experience in Bangladesh,* New York: Oxford University Press, Inc.
4. "Who is Afraid of Big, Bad TV," *Time,* November 23, 1970.
5. Herma Rosenthal, "Sunny Days on Sesame Street," *The Newsday Magazine,* July 17, 1988.

12   ENTREPRENEURIAL GOVERNMENT

1. Approximately $26 billion in current dollars and about 1 percent of the country's GDP at the time
2. Cynthia C. Kelly, ed., *The Manhattan Project: The Birth of the Atomic Bomb in the Words of its Creators, Eyewitnesses, and Historians* (New York: Black Dog & Levanthal, 2007), 161 (as quoted from "In the Matter of J. Robert Oppenheimer," [United States Atomic Energy Commission, June 12, 1954]).
3. Harry S. Truman, "Statement Announcing the Use of the A-Bomb at Hiroshima, August 6, 1945," *Public Papers of the Presidents: Harry S. Truman* (Harry S. Truman Library & Museum, Independence, Missouri).

13 GOVERNMENT MATTERS

1. Richard Tedlow. *Andy Grove: The Life and Times of an American*. New York: Penguin Group, Portfolio Books, 2006, 64.

14 INNOVATE OR DIE

1. *The Global Competitiveness Report 2009-2010 – World Economic Forum.*

SELECTED BIBLIOGRAPHY

Alderman, John. *Sonic Boom: Napster, MP3 and the New Pioneers of Music.* Cambridge, MA: Perseus Publishing. 2001.

American Made: Howard Schultz. CNBC, April 17, 2006. Burrelles Luce.

Ante, Spencer. *Creative Capital: Georges Doriot and the Birth of Venture Capital.* Boston: Harvard Business School Publishing, 2008.

Armstrong, David. "The Segway: Bright Idea, Wobbly Business." *Wall Street Journal*, February 12, 2004.

Auleta, Ken. *Google: The End of the World as We Know It.* New York: Penguin Press, 2009.

Beer, Michael. *Apple Computer (A): Corporate Strategy and Culture.* Harvard Business School Publishing case 9-495-044, February 11, 1997.

Bentley, Rick. "Playboy's Secret Is Not So Dirty." *The Fresno Bee,* December 7, 2003.

Bianco, Anthony. "Power On Wall Street: Drexel Burnham Is Reshaping Investment Banking, and U.S. Industry." *Business Week*, July 7, 1986.

Bird, Kai, and Martin J. Sherwin. *American Prometheus: The Triumph and Tragedy of J. Robert Oppenheimer.* New York: Vintage Books, 2005.

———. "Building the Bomb." *Smithsonian* 88–96 (August 2005).

Brands, H.W. *Masters of Enterprise: Greats of American Business, from John Jacob Astor and J.P. Morgan to Bill Gates and Oprah Winfrey.* New York: The Free Press, 1999.

Brown, John Seeley. Personal interview, January 18, 2007.

Bruck, Connie. *The Predators' Ball: The Junk Bond Raiders and the Man Who Staked Them.* New York: The American Lawyer/Simon & Schuster, 1988.

Burns, Greg. "Adventures in the Skin Trade: Playboy Enterprises Shunned Explicit Sex and Nearly Drowned in Red Ink." *Chicago Tribune,* October 16, 2005.

Burns, Kevin, director. *Hugh Hefner: American Playboy Revisited.* Produced by A & E Television Networks and 20th-Century Fox Television, 2001.

Bygrave, William D., and Jeffry A. Tim. *Venture Capital at the Crossroads.* Boston: Harvard Business School Press, 1992.

Bylinsky, Gene. "General Doriot's Dream Factory." *Fortune* (August 1967), 103.

Car Crash: The DeLorean Story. Mint Productions, BBC, May, 2004.

Chiappini, Rudy, ed. *Christo and Jeanne-Claude*. London: Thames & Hudson [distributor], 2006.

Christiansen, Clayton. *The Innovator's Dilemma: When New Technologies Cause Great Firms to Fail*. Boston: Harvard Business School Press, 1997.

Cohen, Muriel. "Street Smarts: By Combining Education and Entertainment, *Sesame Street* Has Entranced a Generation." *The Boston Globe*, October 29, 1989.

Collier, Christopher, and James Lincoln. *Decision in Philadelphia: The Constitutional Convention of 1787*. New York: Ballantine Books, 1986.

Cooney, Joan Ganz. 1998. Interview #3: Carnegie Corporation of New York Oral History Project. http://www.columbia.edu/cu/lweb/digital/collections /oral hist/carnegie/video-interviews/#cooney.

Corliss, Richard. "That Old Feeling: Your Grandfather's Playboy." *Time,* January 3, 2005.

Cringely, Robert, writer/producer. *The Triumph of the Nerds: The Rise of Accidental Empires*. Documentary film by Oregon Public Broadcasting. PBS, June 1996.

DeLong, Thomas J., and Vineeta Vijayaraghavan. *Cirque du Soleil*. Harvard Business School Publishing, Case 9-403-006, October 15, 2002.

DeLorean, John interview by Robert Scheer. *Playboy* (October 1985).

DeLorean Motor Company. Form S-2 registration statement. January 2, 1977.

Drucker, Peter F. *Innovation and Entrepreneurship: Practice and Principles*. New York: Harper Collins, 1985.

———. "The Discipline of Innovation." *Harvard Business Review* (November–December 1998).

Duval, Jean-Philippe, director. *A Baroque Odyssey*. Cirque du Soleil Productions, 1994.

Egan, Philip. *Design and Destiny: The Making of the Tucker Automobile*. Orange, CA: On the Mark Publications, 1993.

Ellis, Joseph J. *Founding Brothers: The Revolutionary Generation*. New York: Alfred A. Knopf, 2000.

Evans, Harold. *They Made America: From the Steam Engine to the Search Engine, Two Centuries of Innovators*. New York: Little, Brown and Company, 2004.

Evans, Harold. "The Eureka Myth." *Harvard Business Review* (June 2005).

Federal Express S-1 registration statement, 1978.

Fineberg, Jonathan David. *Christo and Jeanne-Claude: On the Way to the Gates*. New Haven: Yale University Press, 2004.

Fischel, Daniel. *Payback: The Conspiracy to Destroy Michael Milken and His Financial Revolution*. New York: Harper Business, 1995.

Florida, Richard. "America's Looming Creativity Crisis." *Harvard Business Review* (October 2004).

Frock, Roger J. *Changing How the World Does Business: FedEx's Incredible Journey to Success, the Inside Story*. San Francisco: Berritt Koehler. 2006.

Fromson, Brett Duval. "Did Drexel Get What It Deserved?" *Fortune,* March 12. 1990.

Fulmer, William E., and Robert F. Fulmer. Revised by Jeanne Lidtka. *Walt Disney Productions: The Walt Years (A).* Darden Business Publishing, University of Virginia *UVA-BP-0332 193.*

Gabler, Neil. *Walt Disney: The Triumph of the American Imagination.* New York: Vintage Books, 2006.

Gompers, Paul A. "A Note on the Venture Capital Industry." Harvard Business School Publishing, case 9-295-065, July 12, 2001.

Gompers, Paul, and Josh Lerner. *The Venture Capital Cycle.* Cambridge: The MIT Press, 1999.

Gordon, Perry, and Minda Zetlin. "How Bad Managers Doomed Drexel." *Management Review,* July 1, 1990.

Gordon, Robert Steele. *An Empire of Wealth: The Epic History of American Economic Power.* New York: Harper Collins, 2004.

Gosling, F. G. "The Manhattan Project: Making the Atomic Bomb." Washington, D.C.: United States Department of Energy, January 1999.

Greenwald, John. "Predator's Fall." *Time,* February 26, 1990.

Groueff, Stephane. *Manhattan Project: The Untold Story of the Making of the Atomic Bomb.* Boston: Little Brown & Co., 1967.

Groves, Leslie R. *Now It Can Be Told: The Story of the Manhattan Project.* New York: Harper & Brothers, 1962.

Hamemesh, Richard G., and David Kiron. "Managing Segway's Early Development." Harvard Business School Press, case 9-804-065 [revised], September 15, 2004.

Hargadon, Andrew. *How Breakthroughs Happen: The Surprising Truth about How Companies Innovate* Boston: Harvard Business School Press, 2003.

Harris, Jeffrey A., Columbia Business School CaseWorks. http://www4.gsb .columbia.edu/caseworks.

The Human Transporter (ID#090313). August 7, 2009.

It Takes a Village. (ID#090318). December 1, 2009.

The Hub. (ID#090319). December 1, 2009.

A Walk in the PARC. (ID#090321). December 1, 2009.

The Street. (ID#090322). December 1, 2009.

The Playboy. (ID#090324). December 1, 2009.

After Dark. (ID#090325). December 1, 2009.

The District. (ID#090328). December 1, 2009.

The Predator. (ID#090329). December 1, 2009.

Heath, Robert. director. *Hugh Hefner, Once Upon a Time.* Playboy Home Video, 1993.

Heilemann, John. "Machine of Dreams." *Vanity Fair* (May 2002).

Hellman, Peter. "Street Smart: How Big Bird & Co. Do It." *3-2-1 Contact* (November 23, 1987): 48–53.

Hennessy, Julie. *'Apple Computer, Inc. Think Different, Think Online Music'*. Kellogg School of Management case KEL-065, January 1, 2004.

Henry, Gordon M. "Dark Clouds over Wall Street." *Time,* May 26, 1986.

Hiltzik, Michael A. *Dealers of Lightning: Xerox PARC and the Dawn of the Computer Age.* New York: Harper Collins, 1999.

Hsu, David H., and Martin Kenney. "Organizing Venture Capital: The Rise and Demise of American Research & Development Corporation, 1946–1973." *Oxford Journals* 14, no. 4 (December 2004): 579–616.

Hunter, Trevor, and Tammy Smith. *Napster and MP3: Redefining the Music Industry.* Ivey Publishing, Richard Ivey School of Business (901M02), June 28, 2000.

Johnson, Jeff. "The Xerox Star: A Retrospective." *IEEE Spectrum* 22, no. 9 (1989): 11.

Johnson, Mark W., Clayton M. Chrstensen, and Henning Kagermann. "Reinventing Your Business Model." *Harvard Business Review* (December 2008).

Josephson, Matthew. *Edison: A Biography.* New York: John Wiley & Sons, 1959.

Kelly, Cynthia C., ed. *The Manhattan Project: The Birth of the Atomic Bomb in the Words of Its Creators, Eyewitnesses, and Historians.* New York: Black Dog & Leventhal, 2007.

Kemper, Steve. *Code Name Ginger: The Story Behind Segway and Dean Kamen's Quest to Invent a New World.* Cambridge: Harvard Business School Press, 2003.

Kim, W. Chan and Renee Mauborgne. *Blue Ocean Strategy: How to Create Uncontested Market Space and Make Competition Irrelevant.* Boston: Harvard Business School Publishing Corporation, 2005.

Kirschner, Scott. "Breakout Artist." *Wired* (September 2000).

Klein, F.C., and Laing, J. R. "Playboy's Slide: Hotel Losses, Decline in Circulation Weakens Hugh Hefner's Empire." *Wall Street Journal,* April 13, 1976.

Klein, Maury. *The Change Makers from Carnegie to Gates: How the Great Entrepreneurs Transformed Ideas into Industries.* New York: Times Books, 2003.

Koehn, Nancy F. *Brand New: How Entrepreneurs Earned Consumers' Trust: From Wedgwood to Dell.* Boston: Harvard Business School Press, 2001.

Koehn, Nancy. *Entrepreneurial History: A Conceptual Overview.* Harvard Business School Publishing, case 9-801-368, February 9, 2001.

Koehn, Nancy. *Howard Schultz and Starbucks Coffee Company.* Harvard Business School Publishing, case 9-801-361, September 30, 2005.

Kressel, Dr. Henry and Thomas Lento. 2007. *Competing for the Future: How Digital Innovations are Changing the World.* New York: Cambridge University Press

Kron, David. *Napster.* Harvard Business School Publishing, case 9-801-219, March 29, 2001.

Kuran, Peter, director. *Trinity and Beyond: The Atomic Bomb Movie.* Visual Concept Entertainment. 1995.

Lagace, Martha. "Not a Scooter, Not a Vehicle: Make Way for Segway." *Harvard Business School Newsletter*, Februay 25, 2002.

Lanouette, William. "Bumbling toward the Bomb." *Bulletin of the Atomic Scientists* 45, no. 7 (September 1989).

Levin, Hillel. *Grand Delusion: The Cosmic Career of John DeLorean*. New York: Viking Press, 1983.

Lovecock, Christopher. *Federal Express: Early History*. Harvard Business School Publishing, case 9-804-095, November 18, 2003.

Lovecock, Christopher. *Federal Express (A)* Harvard Business School Publishing, case 9-577-042, April 1, 1983.

Mandelbaum, Michael. *Democracy's Good Name: The Rise and Risk of the World's Most Popular Form of Government*. New York: Public Affairs, 2007.

MAUD Committee. *Report on the Use of Uranium for a Bomb: Outline of Present Knowledge*, March 1941.

Maysles, Albert, director. *Christo & Jeanne-Claude: 5 Films*. Maysles Film Production, 2004.

McCraw, Thomas K., ed. *Creating Modern Capitalism: How Entrepreneurs, Companies, and Countries Triumphed in Three Industrial Revolutions*. Boston: Harvard University Press, 1995.

Menn, Joseph. *All The Rave: The Rise and Fall of Shawn Fanning's Napster*. New York: Crown Books, 2003.

Merriden, Trevor. *Irresistible Forces: The Business Legacy of Napster and the Growth of the Underground Internet*. Mankato, MN: Capstone Publishing, 2001.

Monaco, Don. "Cooney & the Kids." *Look* (November 18, 1969).

Moore, Geoffrey. "Darwin and the Demon: Innovating within Established Enterprises." *Harvard Business Review* (July–August 2004).

Nichols, Kenneth D. *The Road to Trinity*. New York: William Morrow, 1987.

Owen, David. *Copies in Seconds: How a Lone Inventor and an Unknown Company Created the Biggest Communication Breakthrough since Guttenberg, Chester Carlson and the Birth of the Xerox Machine*. New York: Simon & Schuster, 2004.

Owen, David. "Copies in Seconds." *The Atlantic Monthly* (February 1986).

Packard, David. *The HP Way: How Bill Hewlett and I Built Our Company*. New York, NY: Harper Business, 1995.

Pake, George E. "Research at Xerox PARC: A Founder's Assessment." *IEEE Spectrum* 22, no. 10 (1985): 54–61.

Parks, Louis B. "Hugh Hefner's Playboy Magazine Turns 50." *Houston Chronicle*, December 14, 2003.

Pearson, Charles T. *The Indomitable Tin Goose: The True Story of Preston Tucker and His Car*. New York: Abelard-Schuman, 1960.

Pearson, Charles T. 1946. "That Car." *Pic* (January 1946).

Pellet, Jennifer. "Finding the Secret Sauce for Success." *Chief Executive* (October 1, 2004).

Perry, Tekla S. "Inside the PARC: The Information Architects." *IEEE Spectrum* 22, no. 10 (1985).

Perez, Carlota. *Technological Revolutions and Financial Capital: The Dynamics of Bubbles and Golden Ages.* Cheltenham, UK: Edward Elgar, 2002.

Playboy Enterprises Inc. Form 10-K. Filed with the Securities and Exchange Commitssion, March 2009.

Playboy Enterprises, Inc. Prospectus filed with the Securities and Exchange Commission, November 3, 1971.

Polsky, Richard M. *Getting to Sesame Street: Origins of the Children's Television Workshop.* New York: Praeger Publishers (Aspen Program On Communications and Society), 1974.

Rhodes, Richard. *The Making of the Atomic Bomb.* New York: Simon & Schuster, 1986.

Rivlin, Gary. "Segway's Breakdown." *Wired* (March 2003).

Michael J. Roberts and Lauren Barley. "How Venture Capitalists Evaluate Potential Venture Opportunities." Harvard Business School Publishing (HBSP 9-805-0-19), December 1, 2004.

Ronte, Dieter. *Christo and Jeanne-Claude.* London: Philip Wilson Publishers, Ltd., 2004

Rosenthal, Herma. "Sunny Days on Sesame Street." *Newsday Magazine,* July 17, 1988.

Rukstad, Michael G, David J. Collis and Tyrrell Levine. *The Walt Disney Co.: The Entertainment King.* Harvard Business School Publishing, case 9-701-035, March 9, 2001.

Sandler, Linda. "Drexel Burnham Lambert Finds A Niche." *Institutional Investor* (October, 1981).

Schultz, Howard and Dori Jones Yang. *Pour Your Heart into It: How Starbucks Built a Company One Cup at a Time.* New York: Hyperion, 1997.

Scott, Jeff. "Drexel Burnham Lambert: A Ten-Year Retrospective, Part I: The Rise." Unpublished draft (December 14, 2000).

Senor, Dan and Saul Singer. *Start-Up Nation: The Story of Israel's Economic Miracle.* New York: Twelve, 2009.

Sherman, Dan. "The DeLorean Dilemma." *Car and Driver* (July 1981).

Smith, Adam. Interview with Muhammad Yunus. October 13, 2006. http://www.nobelprize.org.

Smith, Douglas K., and Robert C. Alexander. *Fumbling the Future: How Xerox Invented, Then Ignored, the First Personal Computer.* Lincoln, NE: Authors Choice Press, 1999.

Smith, Fred. Interview by Academy of Achievement, May 23, 1998. http://www.achievement.org/autodoc/page/smi0int-1.

Smith, Fred. "How I Delivered the Goods." *Fortune Small Business,* October 1, 2002. "How We Got Started." *Fortune Small Business,* May 25, 2005.

Smith, Fred. Interview. *Charlie Rose,* May 23, 2008.

Sobel, Robert. *RCA.* New York: Stein and Day Publishers, 1986.

Sobel, Robert and David B. Sicilia. *The Entrepreneurs: An American Adventure.* Boston: Houghton Mifflin, 1986.

Stein, Benjamin. *A License to Steal: The Untold Story of Michael Milken and the Conspiracy to Bilk the Nation.* New York: Simon & Schuster, 1992.

Stone, Dan. *April Fools: An Insider's Account of the Rise and Collapse of Drexel Burnham.* New York: Donald J. Fine, Inc. 1990.

Stowe, Rick. Personal interview. March 21, 2005.

Tedlow, Richard S. *Giants of Enterprise: Seven Business Innovators and the Empires They Built.* New York: Collins, 2001.

They Made America. WGBH Boston. Video, 2004.

Tine, Robert. *Tucker: The Man and His Dreams* (novelization of the screenplay by Arnold Schulman and David Seidler). New York: Pocket Books, Simon & Schuster, Inc., 1988.

Torekull, Bertil. *Leading By Design: The IKEA Story.* New York: Harper Business. 1999.

Trimble, Vance. *Overnight Success: Federal Express and Frederick Smith, Its Renegade Creator.* New York: Crown Publishers, 1993.

Truman, Harry S. 1945. Statement Announcing the Use of the A-bomb at Hiroshima, August 6, 1945. Public Papers of the Presidents: Harry S. Truman. Harry S. Truman Library & Museum, Independence, Missouri.

Uttal, Bro. The Lab That Ran Away from Xerox. *Fortune,* September 5, 1983.

Venture Impact: The Economic Importance of Venture Capital–Backed Companies to the U.S. Economy: A Joint Study by the National Venture Capital Association and IHS Global, 2009.

von Hippel, Eric, Stefan Thomke, and Mary Sonnack. "Creating Breakthroughs at 3M." *Harvard Business Review* (September 1, 1999).

Watts, Steven. *Mr. Playboy: Hugh Hefner and the American Dream.* Hoboken, NJ: John Wiley & Sons, 2008.

Yunus, Muhammad, and van Gelder, Sarah. "The End of Poverty: An Interview with Muhammad Yunus by Sarah van Gelder." *YES, A Journal of Positive Futures.* Issue 2 (Spring 1997).

Yunus, Muhammad interview. CNN, November 20, 2007.

Yunus, Muhammad interview. *Charlie Rose,* June 4, 2004.

Yunus, Muhammad. Speech given at the Council of Foreign Relations. November 16, 2006.

Zider, Robert. "How Venture Capital Works." *Harvard Business Review* (November–December 1998): 131–139.

INDEX

HILLSBORO PUBLIC LIBRARIES
Hillsboro, OR
Member of Washington County
COOPERATIVE LIBRARY SERVICES